Citizens Without A State

★★★

Restoring equal rights under the
Constitution of the United States
for 3.6 million U.S. Citizens
in Puerto Rico

★★★

Howard Hills

Visit "Citizens Without A State" Website:
http://www.pr51st.com/citizens-without-state

Citizens Without A State:
Restoring equal rights under the Constitution of the United
States for 3.6 million U.S. Citizens in Puerto Rico

By Howard Hills

ISBN: 978-0-9849504-1-6

Produced by Craig Lockwood.
Typography, cover design and layout by
Craig Lockwood and Michael McCullen.

Pacific-Noir Pulp Press™
1278 Glenneyre St.
Laguna Beach, California
www.Pacific-NoirPulpPress.com

Printed in the United States

Dedication

Jose Celso Barbosa was black, from a poor family in Puerto Rico during Spain's colonial rule in the 19th century. But he was raised with the island's traditional Christian values of hard work and service.

Seizing the opportunity to use his intelligence to rise above the conditions of his humble birth, Barbosa was the first black student admitted to the Jesuit Seminary in Puerto Rico.

Recognized for his exceptional talents, he went on to earn his medical degree at the University of Michigan Medical School, becoming the first medical doctor from Puerto Rico trained in the United States.

Against all conceivable odds he was voted Valedictorian of his medical school class. He returned to serve his people as a renowned medical doctor, also pioneering a system of employer health insurance for workers in Puerto Rico.

During the Spanish-American War he displayed heroism, entering combat zones under fire to care for both Spanish and American wounded. He later went on to serve in Puerto Rico's first Senate, leading the statehood movement, and contributing to the eventual achievement of U.S. citizenship for his people.

In addition to being the founder of Puerto Rico's statehood movement, Barbosa also founded the Republican Party of Puerto Rico, and affiliated it with the National Republican Party.

As a healer, humanitarian, and statesman, Barbosa smashed every barrier and broke every mold to fulfill his own creative potential in service to his people and our nation. It is to his courage and vision of a free and democratic Puerto Rico under a fifty-one star American flag that this project is dedicated.

Foreword
By Dick Thornburgh

During Ronald Reagan's successful presidential campaign in 1980, he actively supported statehood for Puerto Rico, even making an eloquent argument for its admission as the 51st State in the opinion pages of the Wall Street Journal. When he took office in 1989, President George Bush also declared his support for Puerto Rico's admission to statehood in his first State of the Union address.

So it came as no surprise to me that interest in Puerto Rico's political status intensified during the period between 1988 and 1991, when I served as U.S. Attorney General in both the Reagan and Bush administrations. It was on my watch at the Department of Justice that the debate over federal administration of our nation's last large and populous territorial possession culminated in Congressional hearings in the U.S. Senate on Puerto Rico's status.

> "Commonwealth" is a temporary and not fully democratic form of local territorial self-government over purely local civil affairs.

Given persistent confusion and disarray in federal legal policy on the question of Puerto Rico's political status options, I welcomed the request to appear before Congress in 1991. My initial goal was to clarify legal ambiguities about the actual extent of self-government allowed by the so-called "commonwealth" system for administration of local civil affairs in Puerto Rico, under a territorial constitution approved by Congress in 1952.

"Commonwealth" denotes a temporary and not fully democratic form of local territorial self-government over purely internal matters not otherwise governed by federal law. Yet the local political party favoring the status quo in Puerto Rico promoted the legally flawed concept that "commonwealth" status could be "enhanced" to combine features of both statehood and independent nationhood.

This politically unrealistic doctrine—that a "commonwealth" regime for territorial government could be converted into a constitutionally permanent political status and continue indefinitely — had prompted then candidate Reagan to write in his 1980 opinion piece:

"As a 'commonwealth' Puerto Rico is now neither a State nor independent, and thereby has an historically unnatural status."

That frank assessment of the historical ambiguity inherent in Puerto Rico's current political status was confirmed when local votes on political status in 1993 and 1998 turned out to be inconclusive, due to confusing and misleading definitions of the term "commonwealth." With ballots offering a "commonwealth" option that promised the most prized benefits of both statehood and nationhood, without the full burdens of either, it is of little wonder that no status option received a majority in each local referendum held in the last decade of the twentieth century.

Following the 1991 hearing in the U.S. Senate at which I testified as Attorney General, Congress began a long process of defining legitimate status options. Congressional deliberations were accelerated after President Bush issued a directive to promote status resolution for Puerto Rico based on legally valid options. The "Bush Memo" called for "periodic" status votes to confirm whether or not more than 3.5 million U.S. citizens of Puerto Rico continued to consent to their current status or aspired to a new relationship with the United States, based on statehood or nationhood.

Consistent with the 1992 Bush Memo, the U.S. House of Representatives passed a "Puerto Rico Political Status Act" in 1998, which included authorization for the U.S. citizen

Consistent with the 1992
Bush Memo, the U.S. House of
Representatives passed a "Puerto
Rico Political Status Act" in 1998...
for residents of Puerto Rico to
choose among... territorial status,
statehood and nationhood.

★★★

President Clinton renewed and
expanded on the policy of the
Bush Memo in 2000, by issuing
an Executive Order creating the
President's Task Force on Puerto
Rico's Status.

★★★

In 2005, the White House issued a
report by the presidential task force,
which called for a status vote based
on the status options recognized as
compatible with federal law.

residents of Puerto Rico to choose among the options of maintaining their current territorial status, statehood or nationhood. That bill died in the U.S. Senate because of opposition by a coalition of special interests opposed to any change in Puerto Rico's status.

President Clinton renewed and expanded on the policy of the Bush Memo in 2000, by issuing an Executive Order creating the President's Task Force on Puerto Rico's Status. In 2005, the White House issued a report by that task force which called for a vote based on the status options recognized as compatible with federal law.

> **In that historic vote, fifty-four percent voted to end the current status, and sixty-one percent chose statehood.**

Meanwhile, numerous bills to sponsor a status vote were introduced in Congress, prompting debate in committee hearings focused on the constitutionality of various status options. By 2012, the record created in Congress and the Executive Branch provided enough certainty about the definitions of legally valid options that Puerto Rico finally was able to conduct an informed act of self-determination. In that historic vote, fifty-four percent voted to end Puerto Rico's current status and sixty-one percent chose statehood.

Predictably, statehood opponents challenged the certified results of that referendum. A thorough analysis in this book by Howard Hills, based on relevant legal precedents arising from other territorial status votes throughout our history, confirms the legitimacy of the 2012 vote.

The Obama administration also recognized the certified vote count in 2012 as a "clear result" that, at a minimum, justifies a second federally sponsored vote to reconfirm the results of that referendum. Such a vote has been authorized in a law passed by Congress, and signed by the President in 2014, which provides an open-ended commitment of funds to sponsor a referendum based on definitions certified as legally valid by the U.S. Attorney General.

As Hills explains, a final vote affirming majority rule in favor of a new status would be in keeping with U.S. practice and policy in the cases of Hawaii, Alaska, the Philippines and other territories in the modern era. A second federally recognized vote, informed by the results of 2012's local referendum, would also be consistent with international conventions on political rights and self-determination to which the United States is a party.

This is the historical and legal context in which the United States must now address the social, political and legal meaning of the decision by Congress to confer U.S. citizenship on all persons born in Puerto Rico for nearly a century.

These are issues I addressed in a book published in 2007 by the Washington-based Center for Strategic and International Studies, a well-respected non-partisan think-tank. *"Puerto Rico's Future: A Time To Decide"* was not only about Puerto Rico's status, but rather a broad-gauge survey of the history of federal relations with all U.S. territories.

In this new study, Hills, who was my principal collaborator in that CSIS project, brings new light to bear on the flawed and anachronistic federal court rulings and territorial policies that are central to the dilemma of incomplete democratization in Puerto Rico.

Hills casts in stark relief the full implications of failed doctrines underlying current federal territorial law and policy. In doing so, he traces missteps of the U.S. Congress and of the federal courts departing from America's anti-colonial traditions. Most egregious has been the policy of extending U.S. *citizenship* to residents of *unincorporated* territories, but *not* the *rights* accorded to citizens under the U.S. Constitution.

Hills brings new focus to separation of national citizenship from the Constitution, preventing political integration and reducing the meaning of citizenship in the territory to an ability under current federal statutory law to leave and gain equal rights while residing in a State. In doing so, Hills articulates the inescapable truism that *"the primary democratic rights of national citizenship under our Constitution are exercised through State citizenship."*

Specifically, only U.S. citizens of a State admitted to the Union on equal footing with all other States are able to vote in federal elections, and thereby give consent to be governed under the supreme law of the land. Hills argues that *"...conferral of something called 'citizenship' without a mechanism to acquire federal voting rights and equal representation in the federal political process is a cruel historical hoax."*

> Hills articulates the inescapable truism that "the primary democratic rights of national citizenship under our Constitution are exercised through State citizenship."

That glaring truth affects not only Puerto Rico, but also, as Hills describes, four much smaller island territories with populations the size of small cities. For these smaller territories, integration into an existing State, if attainable, is perhaps the most feasible way for their residents to secure citizenship rights equal to those of citizens in the States.

Hills also authoritatively differentiates the plenary power of Congress over territories, which arises under the Territorial Clause of the Constitution, from the distinctly different constitutional sources of Congressional power to govern the District of Columbia, under legal authorities inapplicable to territories.

As Hills explains, Puerto Rico is the last American territory meeting historical criteria for admission to statehood. Resolution of Puerto Rico's status is the first and most important step toward correction of failed federal territorial law and policy conferring citizenship under the Territorial

Clause without first determining if full integration into the Union is intended.

Hills makes the case that our national character and conscience requires us to correct the failed policy conferring national citizenship in territories not also incorporated into the Union. For the citizens of such territories, only integration into the political order of statehood can end the denial of equality.

This book challenges Americans today to do precisely what the authors of our liberty, during the 1770's and 1780's were trusting us to do. The patriots of revolutionary times were counting on us to understand the ordered scheme of liberty and equality at the core of America's system of constitutional federalism, and to defend both in perpetuity.

Hills' narrative calls on us to redeem the promise of U.S. citizenship in Puerto Rico by making the rights of State citizenship possible for Puerto Rico if that is the status the people of Puerto Rico choose on terms accepted by Congress. In doing so we will restore the meaning of equal rights and duties of citizenship throughout the entire Union.

If we are not willing to honor the choice of our fellow citizens in Puerto Rico to seek out statehood, then we need to face the reality that national citizenship conferred by Congress in a large and populous territory no longer carries with it the promise, or even the hope, of equal rights for such citizens.

Hills calls upon Congress to "deconstruct" institutionalization of an anomalous anti-democratic territorial doctrine in Puerto Rico, based on permanent

> Hills argues, "...conferral of something called 'citizenship' without a mechanism to acquire federal voting rights and equal representation in the federal political process is a cruel historical hoax."

A person in a U.S. territory with national citizenship, but not state citizenship, is denied the most fundamental rights in the domestic community of states.

★ ★ ★

If we are not willing to honor the choice of our fellow citizens to seek out Statehood, then we need to face the reality that national citizenship conferred by Congress no longer necessarily carries with it the promise or even the hope of equal rights.

- Dick Thornburgh

disenfranchisement of U.S. citizens in a territory meeting the threshold indicia of readiness for statehood. To do otherwise would result in a permanent subclass of what Hills aptly calls "citizens without a State."

It is clearly established and accepted that a person who is "stateless" under international law is denied fundamental rights of nationality in the community of nations. What Hills explains is that, under the U.S. system of constitutional federalism, a person in a U.S. territory with national citizenship, *but not State citizenship*, is denied the most fundamental rights in the domestic community of States.

Hills' compelling argument reveals the inherent contradictions of conferring "citizenship"—our greatest gift—in name only on residents of the territories. As Hills explains, in our history and tradition, whenever the United States has exercised sovereignty over a large and populous territory, national citizenship always has led to equal rights that can be secured only by State citizenship. That result alone is fully consistent with the original intent of the Founders, as embodied in the Constitution and the Northwest Ordinance.

As Hills further explains, the alternative to statehood for a large and populous territory like Puerto Rico is independent nationhood, rather than the current commonwealth status, which leaves the millions of U.S. citizens who live in Puerto Rico without full self-government. If U.S. soverenty is to continue, only equal rights of national and State citizenship can bestow upon the residents of Puerto Rico the full measure of democracy that is consistent with our nation's founding principles.

Dick Thornburgh is a former two-term Governor of Pennsylvania, Attorney General of the United States under Presidents Reagan and George H.W. Bush, and Undersecretary General of the United

Nations. He is currently counsel to the law firm of K & L Gates, LLP, resident in Pittsburgh, PA.

Prologue

For one hundred and fifteen years Puerto Rico, her islands and people, have thrived as a distinctly accomplished American community within the national borders of the United States.

By act of Congress in 1917, every person born on American soil in Puerto Rico is a U.S. citizen.

Yet, unless our fellow citizens leave home and move to a State, or Puerto Rico becomes a State, citizenship as we know it under the U.S. Constitution is out of reach in America's last large and populous territorial possession.

Those who only have known the blessings of living in our fifty States take for granted every day civil and political rights denied in Puerto Rico because it remains a U.S. territory instead of a State.

For more than three and a half million U.S. citizens Puerto Rico is home, where people go about "the pursuit of happiness" just as we do in our own hometowns across the nation. The jarring difference is that citizens in Puerto Rico do not have equal rights under the laws of our nation when it comes to "pursuit of happiness" issues like taxes, fighting wars, or health care.

Can you imagine waking up tomorrow, owing allegiance to the U.S. government under federal law, but without the right to vote in elections for those who make the national laws under which we all live?

What if using your U.S. passport to leave for a foreign country, or relocating to a State that is not your chosen home, were the only choices you had to seek relief and respite from denial of the most important rights of U.S. citizenship?

U.S. citizens in Puerto Rico pay local taxes on local earnings, and the same federal income tax as the rest of us on earnings in the fifty States or foreign countries. Our fellow U.S. citizens residing in Puerto Rico also pay all the same federal Social Security and Medicare payroll taxes as citizens in the States, but benefits are lower for citizens in Puerto Rico than in the States.

Local law is nullified if incompatible with federal law made by Congress, in which Puerto Rico has no democratic representation. In more than a century no federal act denying in Puerto Rico rights of citizenship protected in the States has ever been reversed by a federal court.

Despite the social and economic success of this enterprising people, in 2015 the "commonwealth" territorial regime spiraled toward a condition of fiscal, economic and developmental arrest. This crisis was predicted decades ago as the inevitable outcome of politics in Washington and San Juan obstructing Puerto Rico's economic integration on an equal footing with the States.

No wonder then that so many are joining the exodus leaving for the rights and opportunities of U.S. citizens who live in a State. In the second decade of the second century after our nation's flag was raised over the island, no U.S. citizen should be forced to leave home to live in freedom somewhere else in our nation.

Because there is no true liberty without equality, and our Constitution secures full equality only in States of the Union, national citizenship is not complete citizenship without citizenship in a State.

Unless equality and liberty are to be denied in perpetuity to millions of U.S. citizens, Puerto Rico's full integration into the nation on terms ratified by Congress and the voters of the territory is the only course to redeem under U.S. sovereignty the promise of America in Puerto Rico.

H. H.

01

Puerto Rican Identity and American Democracy

Exploring the new world, Christopher Columbus made landfall at Puerto Rico. Ponce De Leon governed Spain's holdings in the Americas from San Juan, the fabled capital city of Puerto Rico. Today the majestic walls of El Morro that once fortified San Juan against invaders are an ancient landmark, visited by tourists from around the world who vacation in Puerto Rico each year. Now a thriving metropolis, San Juan is the oldest city in the United States.

Puerto Rico became a U.S. territorial possession in 1899, when Spain ceded the island to America in the treaty ending the Spanish-American war. In 1900, Congress enacted a federal statute establishing the first civil government for the territory.

Local elected leaders petitioned for U.S. citizenship, but only if it would lead to statehood, which they understood to be the only non-colonial status under the U.S. Constitution.

In 1917, Congress took what was, historically, the first step leading to statehood by granting U.S. citizenship to all persons born in Puerto Rico. A centennial celebration soon will honor one hundred years of federal territorial law bestowing the blessing of *birthright* citizenship in Puerto Rico.

Today the U.S. citizen population of Puerto Rico is more than *three and half million. Thus, the islands of the territory are home to more of our fellow U.S. citizens than twenty-one of the States in the Union.*[1]

Puerto Rico lies off the southeastern continental border of our nation. The distance between Florida and Puerto Rico is less than half the distance separating California and Hawaii.

Our last large island possession remaining after the territory of Hawaii became a State, Puerto Rico is an epicenter of American interests extending our nation's sovereign boundaries into strategic sea-lanes between the Western Hemisphere and Europe.

In nearly a century since Congress conferred U.S. citizenship in Puerto Rico, federal law and policy gradually led to *de facto* incorporation of Puerto Rico into our nation.

> A centennial celebration soon will honor one hundred years of federal territorial law bestowing the blessing of birthright citizenship in Puerto Rico.

---

1   Another four million U.S. citizens from Puerto Rico live throughout the fifty States. The total population of U.S. citizens from Puerto Rico on the island and in the States is greater than the populations in thirty-eight of the fifty States.

FACT:

Residents in Puerto Rico pay the same federal payroll taxes for Social Security and Medicare as their fellow citizens in the States, but Congress provides a lower level of benefits and services for citizens in the territory compared to the States.

FACT:

The U.S. citizens of Puerto Rico serve in America's military at a far higher rate than most States. They pledge allegiance to our flag, live under our form of government, and the statutes approved by Congress are the supreme law of the land, as in the nation as a whole.

In most respects U.S. governance of Puerto Rico for more than a century has been a political, economic and cultural success story, especially when civil freedoms, prosperity and quality of life in Puerto Rico are contrasted with comparable island societies in the region, and around the world. Despite having been denied the full advantages of political and economic integration with the United States, the territory thrived.

Thirty-two U.S. territories that became States of the Union prospered under the American model for territorial development before admission to the Union. The territory has already achieved the blessings of "virtual statehood" in many ways.

As a result, the political, social, economic and cultural bonds between the U.S. citizens of Puerto Rico and the rest of our nation are stronger today than those that existed for most of the other thirty-two territories that became States between 1796 and 1959.

In that historical context it is hard for most Americans to understand why, after one hundred and fifteen years of U.S. rule, the territory of Puerto Rico still has not been admitted to the union as a state.

FACT:

Washington's failure to proceed with full constitutional incorporation opening the door to statehood is historically unprecedented and politically anti-democratic.

FACT:

The result has been perpetuation of an anachronistic territorial status with only a "commonwealth" system of limited self-government in the administration of local civil affairs.

A local territorial constitution was adopted in 1952, but all local law is subject to supremacy of federal law made by Congress, in which the millions of voters in the territory, all U.S. citizens residing in the island territory, have no voting representation.

FACT:

Our fellow U.S. citizens in the territory do not vote for the President, and the federal courts have ruled that territorial status does *not* convey *equal* civil rights taken for granted by citizens in the States.

FACT:

1980 the U.S. Supreme Court upheld federal policy denying equal federal benefits to citizens in Puerto Rico compared to citizens in the States, ruling it was a legitimate exercise of Congressional power over territories. The court held discrimination impermissible in States was allowed because the Constitution applies in Puerto Rico only as determined by Congress.

U.S. citizens in Puerto Rico pay federal taxes on income earned in the fifty States of the Union, or outside the USA. A limited exemption from paying federal taxes on income earned on the island is offset by local income taxes that make the combined federal and local tax rate as high or higher than most States of the Union. Yet, that limited exemption from federal taxation is used by some in Congress and the local political party favoring the status quo as justification for continuation of Puerto Rico's colonial status.

In short, the present status constitutes institutionalized denial of full democratic self-government and equal U.S. citizenship rights at the local and national levels.

Despite decades of federal subsidization, in 2015 Puerto Rico reached the brink of bankruptcy. The "commonwealth" model of territorial rule has produced what now could become a failed client State.

Puerto Rico's uncertain political status has impeded a robust and diversified local economy and vibrant entrepreneurial culture. The current failed "commonwealth"

In short, the present status constitutes institutionalized denial of full democratic self-government and equal U.S. citizenship rights at the local and national levels.

regime is propped up by billions in annual federal taxpayer funded programs and service, but that is no substitute for sustained private sector-led wealth production and growth.

In contrast, history shows that other economically underperforming territories were able to breakthrough to sustained growth and prosperity only after the stability and security of statehood was secured. Thus, it no longer is deniable that the "commonwealth" regime is unsustainable and dying a slow economic death.

Yet, the anti-statehood party in Puerto Rico is aligned with island and mainland political and corporate special interests opposed to any change of status. Millions are spent annually on both anti-statehood and anti-independence propaganda and political campaign spending aimed at Congress and the public.

The ideological illusion that "commonwealth" can be a non-territorial status combining features of statehood and separate nationhood has been discredited. Still, the anti-statehood party in the territory remains politically competitive due to its' historical role as one of two major parties.

The anti-statehood "commonwealth" party has presided over the collapse of the territorial economy, and even its anti-statehood allies in Congress who tout the "commonwealth" party-line don't take it seriously. The myth of a non-territorial "commonwealth" is simply a political tactic to impede the progress of the pro-statehood movement.

Puerto Rico's convergence with the U.S. national standard of living can be achieved only through full economic and fiscal integration. Clearly, the time has come to transition from a territorial status fostering dependency instead of growth, and to end our nation's century long experiment governing a large U.S. citizen population outside the framework of the U.S. Constitution.

02

Consent of the Governed

Today, Puerto Rico remains our nation's only geographically large and demographically populous territory, with a current condition of inequality and political disenfranchisement that has persisted for more than nine decades.

This protracted and indefinite denial of voting rights in federal elections, less-than-equal civil rights, and the lack of voting representation in Congress has created a dilemma that must be resolved by instituting government by consent of the governed at the federal level.

Given that governance by the sovereign with democratic consent of the people is the only form of government we as a nation recognize to be just, in both its inception and its mechanisms to realize the will of the people, the perpetuation of territorial status for Puerto Rico is vexatious to American constitutionalists. Perpetual subjection to U.S. law, without fully meaningful consent given in the manner provided in the Constitution, is legally and politically anti-democratic and repugnant to the principles of the Declaration of Independence.

For a century now we have smugly considered ourselves clever enough to devise a substitute set of benefits to compensate for denial of justice, unsuccessfully rationalizing an essentially colonial condition, unconvincingly citing as validation the complicity of those in the colony who profit by it.

No one is really fooled by gimmicks like giving elected territorial representatives in the lower House of Congress votes in committees but not on actual passage of legislation. Indeed, the farce of giving territorial representatives a vote that doesn't count if it would decide an issue adds insult to the injury of disenfranchised status. Since all federal laws can be amended before adoption, only a vote on final passage of all laws will end the colonial condition that currently disenfranchises the U.S. citizens of Puerto Rico.

Federal territorial policy leaders and their functionaries also cite as justification for open-ended undemocratic imperial rule, decades of confused and inconclusive local votes on formulations of the political status question politically contrived to prevent informed self-determination on the real options.

In the halls of Congress and corridors of the executive departments there too often has been self-satisfied gloating when ambivalent and ambiguous federal and local initiatives to define politically and legally viable status options inevitably fail.

After decades of apathy and sabotage of informed self-determination at the federal level, the U.S. citizens of the territory finally seized the initiative and made history in 2012.

FACT:

In a 2012, locally sponsored status vote, a clear majority of our fellow U.S. citizens in Puerto Rico freely and democratically expressed their aspirations to complete the island's integration into our nation by becoming the fifty-first State of the Union.

FACT:

An impressive seventy-eight percent of registered voters participated in the referendum, in which fifty-four percent voted to seek a new political status rather than continue to be a U.S. territory. On a separate ballot question sixty-one percent voted for statehood instead of independence as a permanent status.

FACT:

2012's vote for statehood on the second question was greater than the vote for Puerto Rico's current status on the first—leaving no reasonable doubt about the meaning of the vote.

Of course, for the anti-statehood political party in Puerto Rico and its allies in Washington, a robust political debate about

2012's results continued unabated. In seeking to deny the clear meaning of the certified vote for statehood, the anti-statehood party favoring the current status under the "commonwealth" banner joined forces with the small independence party, even though the independence party has not won more than 5% of the vote in a status referendum.

This anti-statehood alliance went so far as to assert that ballots left blank on the choice between statehood and nationhood should be counted as votes against statehood!

Corporate special interests that benefit financially from federal and local laws sustaining the status quo funded an orchestrated lobbying campaign in Congress. Anti-statehood lobbyists influenced U.S. Senators to ignore the certified vote results, and declare statehood had been approved by only forty-four percent of the voters!

Again, this campaign of deceitful disinformation was based on the fiction that blank ballots on the statehood versus nationhood question were a *rejection* of statehood. Yet, under U.S. and international election law blank ballots cannot be counted unless provided by law and ballot instructions to voters.[2]

More importantly, the number of ballots that were not left blank on the statehood question, and which voters marked in favor of

> Blank ballots can't somehow be "counted" against statehood for purposes of political rhetoric or ideological propaganda, because numerically statehood won over the current status.

---

2   Congress, the federal courts and the United Nations upheld results of the referendum on political status treaties between the U.S. and the Republic of the Marshall Islands in 1983, without counting blank ballots on a second question most voters declined to answer after making their choice on the first ballot question. The same policy against counting blank ballots has applied in each territory admitted to the Union in which a status referendum was conducted.

statehood, was greater than the number of votes cast on the first ballot question for the status quo. So, affirmative marked votes for statehood beat affirmative marked votes on the separate up or down ballot question on continuation of the current relationship between the U.S. and Puerto Rico.

This has two transcendent meanings. First, it means blank ballots can't somehow be "counted" against statehood for purposes of political rhetoric or ideological propaganda, because numerically *statehood* still won over the current status. Secondly, it means that speculation about how the "commonwealth" regime could be reformed or nationhood could become a viable option is no longer supported by a majority.

The clearly expressed will of the people calls for an end to the status quo, no matter what federally subsidized fiscal gimmicks are proposed to prop it up. Voters have rejected separate nationhood because it means U.S. citizenship will end.

Clearly, 2012's vote for statehood ends decades of inconclusive plebiscites on status alternatives based on local politics rather than the Constitution or political and economic realities.

FACT:

Local status votes in 1993, and 1998, were based on inaccurate and misleading status option definitions making false promises to voters, who were smart enough to deny even the too-good-to-be-true "commonwealth" option a majority.

The 2012 vote was based on accurately and fairly defined status options, and the results now eclipse all previous votes. This historic vote may well be confirmed by subsequent votes sponsored by the local government or by Congress in Washington, but the 2012 vote is legally and politically sufficient to stand-alone as a valid act of democratic self-determination.

Unless the people rescind approval of statehood by a subsequent vote, the 2012 vote stands as an affirmative vote for statehood, legally and politically a more clear democratic mandate than the votes on statehood in several territories that became States.[3]

The only historical and legal meaning that can be given to this vote is that the people withdrew consent to continuation of the current status. Now statehood deserves a clean up-or-down vote without confusing political spin and legal advocacy of questionable validity concerning "commonwealth" or sovereign nationhood.

> This historic vote may well be confirmed by subsequent votes sponsored by the local government or by Congress in Washington, but the 2012 vote is legally and politically sufficient to stand-alone as a valid act of democratic self-determination.

---

3   In the Territory of Nebraska's only status referendum a minority of 47% voted for statehood, but after seven years it still became a state. In Colorado's only referendum, statehood lost, garnering only 45% of the vote. Congress passed a statehood enabling act for Wisconsin after statehood received only 22% of the vote.

Voters clearly rejected continued territory status and separate nationhood, the non-statehood alternatives advanced by local highly partisan anti-statehood interests in 2012. After decades in which legally and politically unrealistic "commonwealth" status options were promoted, voters were presented with true choices, and voters chose statehood.

Again, another referendum with multiple options would become necessary *only* if voters reversed the 2012 results. For that to come about voters first must *reject statehood* in an up-or-down vote, nullifying the 2012 vote favoring statehood.

03
Restoring America's Anti-Colonial Values

Puerto Rico's definitive 2012 status vote must now be understood in the historical context of our nation's anti-colonial tradition of territorial status resolution.

Specifically, the principle expressed in the Declaration of Independence, holding that *just power of government exists only with consent* was addressed for U.S. territories by the Northwest Ordinance of 1789.

A founding document of our republic, the Northwest Ordinance was conceived and originally written by Thomas Jefferson for the very reason that *only State citizens have federal voting rights and representation under the Constitution.* Accordingly, the Northwest Ordinance provided the original road map for all thirty-two territories populated by U.S. citizens to seek and give consent to permanent union through statehood.

The alternative model for territorial status resolution is *separate nationhood* leading to independence, but the independence faction in Puerto Rico is no more representative of the population than the separatist movements were in Texas, Vermont, Alaska and Hawaii, during the transition to statehood.

Indeed, in the Post-World War Two era, an "independence option" has been offered and accepted by voters only for U.S. governed territories inhabited by foreign aliens rather than U.S. citizens.

Thus, during the twentieth century the U.S. ruled over but did not confer U.S. citizenship in Cuba, the Philippines, Palau, Micronesia and the Marshall Islands, with the result that today each of those territories is a sovereign nation.

In contrast, during the Twentieth Century Congress recognized U.S. citizenship under the constitution for those residing and born in the territories of Arizona, Oklahoma, New Mexico, Alaska and Hawaii. This enabled the citizens of those incorporated territories to enjoy basic due process and equality under the law, but most importantly citizens were able to exercise democratic self-determination leading to statehood.

> **Puerto Rico was the first, and at the time only, territory in U.S. history where Congress conferred U.S. citizenship but did not follow historic as well as legal precedent by providing for democratic self-determination and political integration leading eventually to statehood.**

Puerto Rico was the first, and at the time only, territory in U.S. history where Congress conferred U.S. citizenship but did not follow historic as well as legal precedent by providing for democratic self-determination and political integration leading eventually to statehood.

Only now, after nearly twelve decades of momentous national and world events in which Puerto Rico played significant roles supporting U.S. national interests, it is becoming clear Puerto Rico's status remains unresolved *because confusion in Washington created confusion in Puerto Rico.*

We now can see quite clearly that in their confusion the U.S. Supreme Court, Congress and the Executive Branch somehow lost grasp of the ideas and truths that run through the Constitution and bind citizenship to the principles of equality, liberty and justice for all.

Washington lost its bearings on principles of democracy under law when the Supreme Court treated U.S. citizenship conferred by Congress in Puerto Rico as different from and subordinate to U.S. citizenship conferred by Congress on former non-citizens in territories such as Louisiana, Alaska and Hawaii.

Short-term politics and ambitious, powerful personalities, rather than history, law, and national values, led to an inconsistent citizenship policy and status for Puerto Rico. Congress and the Courts tolerated this deviation from precedent in governing Puerto Rico, even though its political condition and relationship to the federal government was constitutionally indistinguishable from Alaska and Hawaii.

FACT:

Congress exercised the same constitutionally sourced powers over territories in Alaska, Hawaii and Puerto Rico, but treated Puerto Rico in an entirely different and discriminatory way.

In a 1922 Supreme Court ruling[4] that cannot be reconciled with directly applicable Court precedent, U.S. citizenship in Puerto Rico was irrationally *delinked* from application of the Constitution. Congress should have exercised its power over

---

4   Balzac v. Porto Rico (258 U.S. 298), later re-named Balzac v. Puerto Rico after Congress changed spelling of the island's name. See Chapter 9 for in-depth analysis of Balzac ruling.

territories to *restore* the historical meaning of citizenship in the territories going back to the Northwest Ordinance.

Congress, instead, failed.

Congress regrettably embraced the judicially imposed doctrine that citizenship had no bearing on Puerto Rico's political or constitutional status.

This has complicated territorial law and policy by reinforcing the misconception that conferring citizenship in territories is mere political window dressing that had no constitutional consequences.

When the U.S. failed to adhere to the principles of Thomas Jefferson's Northwest Ordinance in Puerto Rico, lost in the fog of politics was clear recognition that the meaning of U.S. citizenship can be fully realized *only through residence in a State of the Union.*

Instead, the Congress has allowed Supreme Court-invented doctrine to suspend application of the Constitution to U.S. citizens who live in Puerto Rico because it is a territory labeled "unincorporated" by judicial edict. At the same time, Congress uncritically accepted the Supreme Court's inconsistent fiat that the Constitution and the promise of statehood applied to citizens in a territory deemed "incorporated" by the Court.

Yet the Court's determinations that Alaska and Hawaii were incorporated were based on conferral of the same U.S. citizenship Congress conferred in Puerto Rico!

The result? Disarray in American territorial law and policy. Not surprisingly, Puerto Rico's internal status politics have reflected the ambiguity and confusion in federal status policy. The irony is that the U.S. citizens of Puerto Rico and their elected leaders have now finally sorted out the disarray in Washington before Congress did.

By conducting the 2012 vote on constitutionally valid options, the U.S. citizens of the territory have defined the anti-colonial status solution that best serves the national interest. This was done at the local level, while the issue was

Congress regrettably embraced
the judicially imposed doctrine
that citizenship had no bearing
on Puerto Rico's political or
constitutional status.

★★★

At the same time, Congress
uncritically accepted the Supreme
Court's inconsistent fiat that the
Constitution and the promise of
statehood applied to citizens in a
territory deemed "incorporated"
by the Court.

Yet the Court's determinations
that Alaska and Hawaii were
incorporated were based on
conferral of the same U.S.
citizenship Congress conferred in
Puerto Rico!

being woefully bungled at the federal level. This is due to anachronistic and legally flawed federal court jurisprudence.

04

Self-Determination: An American Tradition

Fourteen other territories that became states took the initiative to sponsor local self-determination to create a democratic predicate for a statehood petition.[5] Puerto Rico has done its part by sponsoring the 2012 status vote based on constitutionally valid options. With a strong majority of U.S. citizens in Puerto Rico voting for statehood, our nation's anti-colonial history calls on Congress to do its duty.[6]

As it has been every other time a sufficiently large and populous territory has petitioned for statehood, it is within the authority and responsibility of Congress to determine the terms of an act enabling the island territory to take the steps required for a transition to statehood. Or, if Congress decides

---

5 Tennessee, Arkansas, Michigan, Florida, Iowa, Wisconsin, Oregon, Nevada, Nebraska, Colorado, South Dakota, Washington, Alaska, Hawaii

6 Puerto Rico's Elections Commission certified results:
First Question: Continue Present Territorial Status—NO: 53.97% Yes: 46.03%. Second Question: Non-territorial Options—Statehood: 61.16%; Sovereign Free-Associated State, 33.34%; Independence, 5.49%.

Puerto Rico is ready for admission it can adopt an admission act with appropriate transition provisions.

For the Island's three million, five hundred thousand U.S. citizens, the path forward is now clear. Congress can require another vote to confirm the earlier vote for statehood, but it cannot abdicate its duty without doing an injustice to Puerto Rico and eroding our nation's democratic traditions.

Since the current territorial status and "commonwealth" regime received an up-or-down vote in 2012, and lost, an up-or-down vote on statehood now would be sufficient to confirm results of the previous referendum without repeating it.

FACT:

A federally sponsored vote to confirm a *locally* sponsored vote is *not* an uncommon ritual of self-determination in the well-grounded tradition of Jefferson's Northwest Ordinance.

FACT:

Based on the 2012 vote for statehood, in 2014, Congress authorized and funded a referendum to confirm 2012's results

From politically organized but legally non-binding advisory polling before Tennessee's admission in 1796, to 1959's referendum required under Hawaii's admission act, participation in the expression of public opinion to confirm support for statehood has taken many forms.

Congress has often accepted votes to ratify State constitutions and elect statehood delegations to Congress as fully sufficient territorial self-determination for admission.

Thus, fifteen territories have been admitted without a status referendum *per se*. So, Puerto Rico's 2012 vote *more* than satisfies historical precedent for Congress to adopt a statehood enabling act, or even an admissions act, either of which could require a vote to confirm popular support for transition to statehood.[7]

The contemporary narrative in Washington and San Juan must address the status issue—reminding America and the world once again of our nation's higher purpose.

This discussion will revive our individual and collective memory of that moment in history when the founders of the republic were guided to create the U.S. system of constitutional federalism. This edifice was and continues to be based on equal rights and duties for all U.S. citizens that can be secured only through statehood on equal footing with all other states.

In this cause the non-voting U.S. citizens of Puerto Rico and the U.S. Congress are approaching nothing less than a rendezvous with destiny, called to action because our great nation was not meant to govern a subclass of citizens with less than equal rights indefinitely.

Forging a new State in the crucible of the Constitution in a new century will augur nothing less than a restorative affirmation of the American political creed. Enabling millions of U.S. citizens to re-enact the essential ritual of government by consent with equal liberty for all, we most surely will rediscover the transcendental meaning of our nation's consecrated dedication to serve the cause of human freedom.

As President Ronald Reagan predicted in a message from the White House on January 12, 1982:

"In statehood, the language and culture of the island—rich in tradition—would be respected, for in the United States the cultures

---

7 Among 37 states admitted after the original 13, the territories of Ohio, Louisiana, Indiana, Mississippi, Illinois, Alabama, Missouri, California, Minnesota, Kansas, North Dakota, Montana, Idaho, Wyoming, Utah, Oklahoma, New Mexico and Arizona territories were admitted based on petitions by territorial governments and/or approval of state constitutions without a status referendum. The states of Vermont, Kentucky, Maine and West Virginia were carved out of existing states based on petitions expressing popular will, and with permission of the original state's legislature as required by Article IV of the Constitution. Texas alone was neither a territory nor ceded by a state, but rather an independent republic admitted to the union as a State.

of the world live together with pride...To show the world that the American idea can work in Puerto Rico is to show the world that our idea can work everywhere."

That optimistic historical prophecy reminds us that equality and liberty for Puerto Rico will affirm all that is great about America. This is not the vision of Ronald Reagan alone, or merely a policy plank that has appeared in the Republican Party platform for decades.

Rather, it is first and foremost an American idea—the American idea—also given bipartisan expression by national leaders in the Democratic Party. For example, in a Congressional hearing on Puerto Rico's status held on August 1, 2013, U.S. Senator Ron Wyden, Democrat from Oregon and then Chairman of the Senate Committee with legislative jurisdiction over American territories, framed discussion of the 2012 vote for statehood as follows:

"Ninety-five years after receiving U.S. citizenship, Puerto Ricans have achieved leadership in the U.S. military, in business, in the Congress, on the Supreme Court and in many other prestigious positions. But for Puerto Rico to meet its economic and social challenges and to achieve its full potential, this debate over status needs to be settled. Puerto Rico must either exercise full self-government as a sovereign nation, or achieve equality among the States of the Union. The current relationship undermines the United States' moral standing in the world. For a nation founded on the principles of democracy and the consent of the governed, how much longer can America allow a condition to persist in which nearly four million U.S. citizens do not have a vote in the government that makes the national laws which affect their daily lives?"

Seeing America make good on its promise of government by consent in Puerto Rico offers hope to people throughout the world.

Puerto Rico is democracy's current litmus test. In the spirit of our freedom-loving ancestors, the promise of America must now be redeemed in Puerto Rico.

05
National Citizenship in Puerto Rico

Ratified in 1788, the U.S. Constitution took effect in 1789. At that time the Constitution was silent on the subject of citizenship and the rights or power that come with it.

The limits on federal government power over individuals and the States were defined in the Bill of Rights. But the Constitution did not define *who* could claim *national* and *State* citizenship, or how either would be acquired.

Instead, the central affirmative description of the meaning given to citizenship in the Constitution was embodied in the provisions of Article I, Sections 2 and 3, giving citizens of the states the right to be represented in both Houses of the U.S. Congress. The other primary attribute of citizenship under the Constitution was identified in Article II, Section 1, which gives citizens of the states the right to vote in federal elections for electors who choose the President and Vice President in the Electoral College.

Otherwise, the definition of citizenship was left to Congress and the states, *and State citizenship conferred the State-based federal voting rights that in turn secure full rights of national citizenship.* That *affirmative* definition of citizenship powers is to be distinguished from the limits on federal power to regulate the freedom of individuals and the people that are recognized by the Bill of Rights.

The powers of citizenship include the right to vote in federal elections and be represented in Congress, thereby giving or withholding consent to the form of government embodied in the supreme law of the nation. Doing so without undue government regulation of liberty is also an attribute of full citizenship.

In addition to citizenship of the nation and a State under the federal and State constitution, the Constitution provides in Article I, Section 8, that Congress can adopt by federal statutes a "uniform law of naturalization." This is known as the Uniform Naturalization Clause, and primarily it means Congress can provide by law for non-citizen aliens from foreign nations with allegiance to other countries to change their allegiance and become U.S. citizens. In the early period of our history under the Constitution, the Congress exercised this power by passing laws enabling aliens to take an oath of allegiance and become U.S. citizens on terms and conditions prescribed by Congress.

FACT:

The word "naturalized" means that citizenship is granted to a person who did not acquire it at birth, if that person is otherwise eligible under U.S. naturalization laws adopted by Congress.

FACT:

While naturalized citizens have freedoms guaranteed to all citizens, like natural-born citizens the affirmative rights and powers of citizenship can be exercised by new citizens *only upon qualifying for State citizenship.*

FACT:

That *is* the constitutional framework for citizenship in the states that stands in contrast to citizenship and application of the Constitution in territories—especially to the extent federal courts have allowed Congress to govern some territories deemed unincorporated outside the Constitution.

The story of U.S. citizenship in the territories began in 1787, with the Northwest Ordinance, a blueprint for territorial government enacted under the Articles of Confederation.

That road map for application of the Constitution and federal law to citizens in territories was then adopted by the first Congress of the United States, assembled under the Constitution in 1789.

The Northwest Ordinance was enacted as federal law for the very purpose of defining the status and rights of citizens in territory owned or claimed by the federal government but not within a State.

As such, the Northwest Ordinance augmented and complemented the Constitution to provide for incorporation of the territory into the federal union, organization of temporary territorial government, and enforcement of federal law outside the thirteen original States of the Union.

The Northwest Ordinance model of incorporation applied until the territory could develop politically and adopt a republican form of government under a constitution like other States, and thus be admitted to the union as a State.

During the period of incorporation the Constitution applied to the fullest extent deemed practicable by Congress and the courts.

As a result, citizens had basic rights under the Constitution, including due process and equality under law applicable in the territory. That, however, did not include the rights and powers that can be exercised only by citizens of the states. The provisions of the Constitution that apply only to states did not apply in territories, including the right to vote in federal elections, or to be represented in Congress by members of that body able to give consent to law by casting a vote on behalf of other citizens.

As imperfect as incorporation was due to limited application of citizenship powers, including denial of federal voting rights, it enabled territories to establish readiness to join into the more perfect union under the Constitution through statehood. That model was successful for thirty-two territories between 1796 and 1959.

Less perfect than incorporation was the status of *unincorporated territory* invented by the federal courts in 1901, under which the Constitution does not apply to territories that are not incorporated according to the Northwest Ordinance model.

This court-made doctrine of non-incorporation originally applied only to the Philippines, Puerto Rico and Guam after being ceded by Spain after the Spanish-American War.

Federal court rulings known as the Insular Cases began with the 1901 ruling in the case of Downes v. Bidwell, in which

> Less perfect than incorporation was the status of unincorporated territory invented by the federal courts in 1901, under which the Constitution does not apply to territories that are not incorporated according to the Northwest Ordinance model.

the Supreme Court invented the practice of territorial non-incorporation that denied application of the Constitution.

Before the Insular Cases, the courts historically had recognized U.S. citizen-populated territory as permanently under constitutional protection for incorporated territories. Because non-incorporation was a *temporary* form of colonial rule, the courts originally limited its application to territories with *non-citizen* populations.

That worked imperfectly but well enough that non-incorporation was a successful status resolution model for the Philippines during transition to nationhood and independence. But in the 1922 case of Balzac v. Puerto Rico, the courts extended "unincorporated territory" status in Puerto Rico after citizenship was conferred by Congress in 1917.

The story of how the Balzac ruling derailed status resolution based on the historically anti-colonial traditions of federal territorial law reveals the causes and effects of American imperialism run amuck. It is as well the story of how federal territorial law and policy in the Twentieth century failed to redeem the promise of liberty and equality under the Constitution for all those blessed with U.S. citizenship.

However, most of all it is a story of the U.S. Supreme Court exceeding constitutional jurisdiction. Determining the political status of a territory is a political question within the power over territories vested not in the court, but in the Congress under the Territorial Clause.

That was why Article IX of the 1899 treaty with Spain expressly states that "[the] civil rights and political status of the native inhabitants of the territories hereby ceded to the United States shall be determined by Congress."

Yet, the political question of Puerto Rico's future was hijacked by the U.S. Supreme Court in 1922, because the Chief Justice, William Howard Taft, decided that the issues of citizenship, application of the Constitution and political status were too important to be left to Congress.

Stated simply, as a former judge and Governor in the Philippine territory at the time the Insular Cases were handed down, Taft knew more about U.S. territorial law and policy than any of his fellow justices on the U.S. Supreme Court, or for that matter any member of Congress. Unabashedly, Taft imposed his openly espoused colonialist ideas not only on the Court but Congress as well. Chapter 9 of this book is devoted to analysis of Taft's opinion in the Balzac case.

Taft was so shrewd and clever that more than nine decades later Congress and even the courts have never solved the puzzling mystery conjured up in the Supreme Court's 1922 ruling. Nor has Congress or the Court ever clarified how, in the land of the free, the Constitution and the rights it enshrines can be denied in perpetuity to citizens of the nation simply by leaving them indefinitely without citizenship of a State.

06

Advent of "Balzac Citizenship" for Puerto Rico

The U.S. Supreme Court's 1922 ruling in Balzac v. Puerto, separating citizenship from the U.S. Constitution, was politically sudden and legally unprecedented. No sooner had Congress granted U.S. citizenship in 1917, than the court ruled that Puerto Rico would be denied incorporation, and instead remain unincorporated. As a result, for the first time in American history, the rights of citizenship would be determined by Congress, acting outside the sphere of constitutional disciplines and limitations on the powers of government.

For nearly a century this imperial power largely has been unchecked and free of the restraints of the Constitution, as it applies in either the States or even in the "incorporated" territories. Before Balzac, at least conferral of citizenship triggered incorporation with some rights of citizenship under the Constitution, leading eventually to full and equal rights through statehood and the powers of State citizenship.

In contrast, 1922's ruling created "Balzac citizenship," which meant rights of citizenship under the Constitution were held in abeyance and only constitutionally temporary rights conferred by federal statutes—subject to amendment or repeal—applied to citizens in the territory. This also meant that constitutionally defined national citizenship did not apply in unincorporated territories, consistent with non-application of the Constitution generally in territories classified as unincorporated under the Insular Cases.

Before the 14th Amendment was adopted in 1886, federal immigration and naturalization statutes adopted by Congress were the only source of lawful U.S. citizenship. The 14th Amendment created constitutionally defined national citizenship, but it applies only in the States of the Union, along with the rest of the Constitution. But the 14th Amendment did not repeal the Uniform Naturalization Clause in the Constitution, which still allows Congress to grant citizenship by federal law as it did before the the 14th Amendment, including for people in the unincorporated territories.

So a question arises about the purpose, logic and expectations underlying federal policy conferring national citizenship in a territory that has unincorporated status. Why extend citizenship where the Constitution does not apply, in a territory where there is no mechanism for incorporation leading to more perfect union through statehood?

> National citizenship without citizenship in a State is a dead end, a State of limbo, in which the core promise of citizenship, equality, is indefinitely denied. Citizenship without a path to statehood is a cruel hoax.

National citizenship without citizenship in a State is a dead end, a condition of limbo, in which the core promise of citizenship, equality, is indefinitely denied. Citizenship without a path to statehood is a cruel hoax.

It was to avoid that very scenario the first Congress adopted the Northwest Ordinance, which applied the Constitution and led to statehood. Also to avoid that scenario, the court cases that invented the unincorporated territory doctrine applied only to territories populated by non-citizens.

As it had in Louisiana, Alaska and Hawaii, conferral of citizenship meant incorporation leading to statehood. Not for Puerto Rico. Even when Congress conferred citizenship the Balzac court ruled the territory remained unincorporated, and its U.S. citizen population had no rights under the Constitution, but rather only under federal statutes applied to the territory.

Even in the modern era when the Citizenship Clause of the Fourteenth Amendment to the Constitution creates national and State citizenship, Balzac is relied on by Congress to deny fundamental rights of citizenship under the Constitution in the unincorporated territories. Thus, to fully understand the fallacy of the Balzac doctrine one needs to understand the sources and nature of citizenship throughout our history.

07

Sources of U.S. Citizenship Rights

To understand the perverse impact of the 1922 Balzac ruling, knowing the legal nature and sources of U.S. citizenship is vital.

The two exclusive sources of U.S. citizenship are:

1. Direct application of the citizenship provisions added to the U.S. Constitution itself in 1868;

2. Special citizenship statutes passed at the discretion of Congress.

The First of Two Exclusive Sources of Citizenship is the National Citizenship Clause of the U.S. Constitution:

• Section 1 of the 14th Amendment added a National Citizenship Clause to the Constitution, under which a person *"born or naturalized* in the United States, and subject to the jurisdiction thereof"* acquires national citizenship.

• No further action by Congress or a State government is required for a person in a State to be eligible at *birth* or under U.S. *naturalization* law to acquire U.S. citizenship by automatic operation of the National Citizenship Clause.

• The federal courts have ruled that the National Citizenship Clause applies only in a State of the Union, not in a location under U.S. sovereign rule but outside one of the fifty

States, such as an unincorporated U.S. territory, or outside U.S. borders altogether.

• Persons who acquire U.S. national citizenship directly under the National Citizenship Clause at the same time acquire the rights of citizenship in any State of residence, pursuant to the phrase "and of the State wherein they reside," which constitutes a State Citizenship Clause also added to the Constitution by Section 1 of the 14th Amendment.

• The National Citizenship Clause and the State Citizenship Clause operate in tandem to prevent either Congress or the States from impermissibly denying rights of national or State citizenship to any person eligible to enjoy such rights in any State.

The Second of Two Sources of U.S. Citizenship is by Discretionary Act of the U.S. Congress:

• Congress has discretion under the Constitution to grant U.S. citizenship to persons who are not eligible for national citizenship under the 14th Amendment because they are not born or naturalized in a State of the Union.

• For example, under federal law Congress grants U.S. national citizenship to certain children of U.S. citizen parents born outside the borders of the United States.

• In addition, regardless of the citizenship status of parents, the Congress also has granted U.S. citizenship to all persons born in Puerto Rico and three other unincorporated territories that are within U.S. national borders but outside the States of the Union (Guam, Commonwealth of the Northern Marianas and U.S. Virgin Islands).

• Congress can amend or repeal federal laws granting U.S. citizenship to persons born or naturalized outside a State of the Union, limiting or terminating future acquisition of U.S. citizenship by persons born or naturalized outside a State, including those born in an unincorporated U.S. territory such as Puerto Rico.

• In the absence of or after repeal of a federal citizenship law for an unincorporated territory, persons born in the territory would have the status of "nationals," which applies to persons born in unincorporated territories where Congress does not grant U.S. citizenship (currently only American Samoa).

The source of U.S. citizenship for people born in Puerto Rico is statutory naturalization as provided by Congress in the exercise of it powers under the Territorial Clause. Statutory citizenship is granted in Puerto Rico in the same manner as it is to other persons born outside a State of the Union before the 14th Amendment, pursuant to the Uniform Naturalization Clause in Article I, Section 8 of the U.S. Constitution.

Under the "non-incorporation" doctrine of the Insular Cases as applied to U.S. citizens by the 1922 Balzac ruling, residents of Puerto Rico and other unincorporated territories do not have rights of national citizenship under the 14th Amendment as applicable in the States, or as applicable in the in incorporated territories.

08

"Balzac Citizenship" —an Incomplete Status

Historically, however acquired territories owned by the U.S. but not within a State of the Union were in most cases settled and populated by U.S. citizens. Exercising its powers under the Territorial Clause in Article IV, Section 3, Clause 2, Congress organized temporary territorial governments that administered local civil affairs under federal law until the territory and its U.S. citizen population could be deemed ready for transition to statehood.

Under the Northwest Ordinance model for territorial incorporation, the U.S. Constitution applied and general rights of citizenship, due process and equal protection of law applied to the extent not contingent on State citizenship. Full and equal rights and duties of citizenship were attained only when those provisions of the Constitution applicable in the States of the Union—including voting rights and representation - became applicable upon admission of the territory as a State.

The federal courts had the last word on exactly how the Constitution did or did not apply in each territory. But as a general rule the Northwest Ordinance tradition of territorial incorporation was based on the principle that the Constitution applied directly by its own force in each territory, defining the

Full and equal rights and duties of citizenship were attained only when those provisions of the Constitution applicable only in the States of the Union—including voting rights and representation - became applicable upon admission of the territory as a State.

★ ★ ★

The conflict over slavery and the status of tribal natives notwithstanding, the Northwest Ordinance tradition of territorial incorporation with citizenship rights under the Constitution was an anti-colonial doctrine that enabled attainment of equality through statehood. That doctrine was first tested early in the westward expansion by the Louisiana Purchase.

rights and duties of citizenship, as well and the allocation of local and federal powers.

Thus, the rights of the citizens in the territory were limited by the inherent nature of territorial status until the rights that only citizens in the states enjoy were attained. That made full equality through statehood the "manifest destiny" of each incorporated territory.

The conflict over slavery and the status of tribal natives notwithstanding, the Northwest Ordinance tradition of territorial incorporation with citizenship rights under the Constitution was an anti-colonial doctrine that enabled attainment of equality through statehood. That doctrine was first tested early in the westward expansion by the Louisiana Purchase.

For the first time the U.S. had acquired sovereign power over a territory that had not been settled by U.S. citizens. There were compelling cultural, language, political, legal, social, economic and military reasons to adopt an *imperial* rather than *anti-colonial* model for governing Louisiana. Obstacles to integration included pre-existing nationalities of the Spanish and French body politic, as well as the controversy over expansion of slavery into territories expected to become States in the future.

Yet, even in a year that again brought war with our own former colonial masters in Britain, in 1812 Congress exercised both its territorial and naturalization powers in tandem by collective naturalization of the non-citizen territorial population. Because the U.S. was at that time operating in Louisiana under the Northwest Ordinance model and not under the Insular Case or Balzac Doctrine, citizenship meant direct application of the Constitution, incorporation and statehood, which proved the best model for integration of a non-citizen territorial population consistent with anti-colonial principles.

That anti-colonial and anti-imperial model of territorial incorporation based on the rights of U.S. citizenship under the Constitution was the exclusive model for territorial governance, and statehood was the exclusive form of status resolution made available to territories – until 1901, when unincorporated status alternative was invented by the federal high court. At that time thirty-two territories had been incorporated based on citizenship under the Constitution and the Union of States numbered forty-five.[8]

But in that first decade of the Twentieth Century, Congress and the U.S. Supreme Court became beguiled by the idea that America could practice an enlightened "progressive" imperialism. Thus, Congress deviated from the Northwest Ordinance and Louisiana precedents by enacting laws to govern non-citizen populations in the Philippines and Puerto Rico outside the Constitution.

Non-citizen populations of Alaska and Hawaii were granted collective naturalization in 1867, and 1900, respectively, and recognized by the federal courts as incorporated under the Constitution in 1905, and 1903, respectively. However, in the case of Downes v. Bidwell, the U.S. Supreme Court upheld the denial of naturalization and applied its judicially invented doctrine of non-incorporation for non-citizens in the Philippines, Puerto Rico and Guam. That meant for the first time the Constitution did not apply in those territories by its own force.

Under the court-invented doctrine of non-incorporation the territorial residents were classified as "nationals" *but not citizens*! All individual and collective rights were defined as Congress determined, without the restraints on government powers or the ordered scheme of rights under the Constitution that applied in the incorporated territories.

---

8 The following incorporated territories were admitted to statehood after the doctrine of non-incorporation was imposed in Puerto Rico under Insular Cases starting in 1901: Oklahoma (1907), New Mexico (1912), Arizona (1912), Alaska (1959) and Hawaii (1959).

FACT:

The imperialist and colonialist doctrine of non-incorporation in the case of the Philippines was broadly reconciled with American political values by the enactment in 1916, of a territorial de-annexation law initiating that territory's transition to sovereign nationhood and independence. That was a historic step toward restoration of an anti-colonial policy in the Philippines.

Promisingly, five months later Congress took what appeared to be another step to restore the Northwest Ordinance and Louisiana model of territorial incorporation for Puerto Rico. In 1917, Congress enacted a law re-organizing the local government and conferring U.S. citizenship by collective naturalization for the non-citizen population.

FACT:

Upon advent of the Insular Cases and for two decades afterwards, the unincorporated territory doctrine spawned in those rulings applied only to territories populated by non-citizens. Concomitantly, once Downes and the other Insular Cases were decided the only territories classified by the Supreme Court as incorporated were those populated entirely or predominately by U.S. citizens.

That is why it is necessary to recognize that U.S. citizenship—or the denial of it—more than any other criteria was the intrinsic predicate of both incorporated and unincorporated territory status. That is precisely why Justice Brown, in his

> The unincorporated territory doctrine was a pronounced exception to the anti-colonial tradition in U.S. territorial policy going back to the Northwest Ordinance. For that very reason, as Justice Brown revealingly noted, the Supreme Court, in effect, restricted unincorporated territory status to territories with non-citizen populations.

opinion announcing the judgment of the Court in Downes, correctly and tellingly noted that,

"...in the case of Porto Rico and the Philippines...the civil rights and political status of the native inhabitants...shall be determined by Congress. In all these cases there is an implied denial of the right of the inhabitants to American citizenship until Congress by further action shall signify its assent thereto."

Similarly, in his concurring opinion in the Downes case Justice White pointed out that Article III of the 1803 treaty of cession with France provided for U.S. citizenship in territory acquired as part of the Louisiana Purchase. In contrast, White noted, Article IX of the treaty with Spain left the matter of citizenship status in Puerto Rico to be determined by Congress. On that basis, White declared it "obvious" Louisiana was incorporated and Puerto Rico was not (ignoring that under both treaties Congress would still have to enact territorial organic laws to codify the status and rights of the territorial population).

There is little in the Twentieth Century's history of federal territorial affairs that does not reinforce the view that citizenship rather than other factors or criteria constitute the legal and political foundation upon which territorial status was defined as either *incorporated* or *unincorporated* under the doctrine of the Insular Cases.

Some scholars have argued the tortured logic of White's opinion in the Downes

The 1904 case of Gonzales v. Williams defined the status of non-citizens in the unincorporated territories as distinct from either that of a foreign alien or a person of U.S. nationality and citizenship. Rather, non-citizen inhabitants of unincorporated territories were classified as non-citizens "under the national protection of the United States." This was a status at least metaphorically reminiscent of classification as a "subject but not a citizen" of imperial Rome or Britain.

★★★

The only thing worse would be if the unincorporated territory doctrine were to be imposed on U.S. citizens. That is, of course, exactly what happened in 1922, solely because "progressive" imperialists on the Supreme Court, led by Chief Justice Taft, were ideologically opposed to incorporation for Puerto Rico. Taft orchestrated an infamous ruling in the case of Balzac v. Puerto Rico.

ruling was epitomized by his statement that unincorporated territories were "foreign in a domestic sense." Perhaps of greater actual legal import, while also producing cognitive dissonance, Justice White asserted the U.S. Constitution was "operative" but not "applicable" in territories classified by the court's ruling as unincorporated, except as allowed permissively by Congress and the courts on a case-by-case basis.

Rights under the Constitution were made applicable in incorporated territories to promote integration and readiness for statehood. The people in unincorporated territory instead would have whatever status, rights, and degree of participation in government Congress deemed appropriate given its understanding of the social, political and economic condition of the inhabitants.

The unincorporated territory doctrine was a pronounced exception to the anti-colonial tradition in U.S. territorial policy going back to the Northwest Ordinance. For that very reason, as Justice Brown revealingly noted, the Supreme Court, in effect, restricted unincorporated territory status to territories with non-citizen populations.

Thus, although Alaska and Hawaii also were non-contiguous foreign territories previously inhabited by non-citizens and acquired through the exercise of international powers, in its rulings on the political status of those two territories in the early Twentieth Century, the Supreme Court properly held each must be treated as incorporated territory. This was the result in the Mankichi case regarding Hawaii in 1903, and the Rassmussen case regarding Alaska in 1904, both based primarily of the acts of Congress conferring U.S. citizenship in the instruments of annexation.

In contrast, Congress had not conferred citizenship for the territories acquired from Spain when the early Insular Cases were decided. Thus, the mandate of Supreme Court jurisprudence in the Alaska and Hawaii cases was clear, granting citizenship would trigger incorporation and application of the Constitution, and the non-incorporation doctrine of the Insular Cases would apply only in territories where Congress provided for the territorial population to remain non-citizens.

The 1904 case of Gonzales v. Williams defined the status of non-citizens in the unincorporated territories as distinct from either that of a foreign alien or a person of U.S. nationality and citizenship. Rather, inhabitants of unincorporated territories were classified as non-citizens "under the national protection of the United States." This was a status at least metaphorically reminiscent of classification as a "subject but not a citizen" of imperial Rome or Britain.

Thus, to the extent scholars have criticized and even condemned the unincorporated territory doctrine of the Insular Cases as imperialist, colonialist and even racist, at least it can be said that the democratic deficiencies of the federal regimes established by Congress and the Executive Branch to administer the unincorporated territories applied only to non-citizens. The only thing worse would be if the unincorporated territory doctrine were to be imposed on U.S. citizens.

Acquiescence by Congress in the implausible logic of that constitutionally flawed Balzac ruling has led to a century of political limbo for Puerto Rico.

That is, of course, exactly what happened in 1922, solely because "progressive" imperialists on the Supreme Court, led by Chief Justice Taft, were ideologically opposed to incorporation for Puerto Rico. Taft orchestrated an infamous ruling in the case of Balzac v. Puerto Rico, holding that Congress could govern U.S. citizens in Puerto Rico in the same manner as non-citizens in the Philippines under the doctrine of non-incorporation.

Despite vague assurances of "fundamental rights" in the Balzac ruling, never once in nearly one hundred years has Balzac been invoked to restrain or limit any exercise of federal power in Puerto Rico. Acquiescence by Congress in the implausible logic of that constitutionally flawed Balzac ruling has led to a century of political limbo for Puerto Rico.

Territorial statutes conferring U.S. citizenship in Puerto Rico and other territories later were codified in federal immigration and nationality laws. However, future conferral of statutory U.S. citizenship can be terminated or limited, and discrimination not permissible in the States is within the discretion of Congress under Balzac.

09
Curse of the "Happy Imperialist"

William Howard Taft rides carabao while serving as
Governor of the Philippines, circa 1902.

After the U.S. ended Spanish colonial rule in the Philippines and Puerto Rico in 1900, America's first territorial Governors were appointed by the President and tasked to bring enlightened American empire to these societies.

Due to the exuberance of American imperialist optimism, there was little consideration given to the fact that these newly acquired island peoples had been governed by Spain for a period longer than the U.S. had been a nation. Undaunted by history and determined to make history in the American way, the new territorial viceroys from Washington built schools and aligned the U.S. with native oligarchies pandering to American interests.

Lamentably, the first Governor appointed by President McKinley in the Philippines also found himself waging war against Philippine independence forces.

This indigenous people's army had been battling the Spanish regime from which the U.S. had liberated the territory in the name of freedom. But the nationalists turned on the U.S. when it became clear that America intended to impose its own "progressive" brand of imperial rule.

Thus, only after killing tens of thousands of Filipino insurgents and sympathizers, and defeating the independence movement, would the U.S. then blithely renounce any intentions of annexation, and triumphantly declare its enlightened and benevolent support for Philippine independence!

During this early period governing territories populated by non-citizens under the Insular Cases, the first Governor of the Philippines, William Howard Taft, referred to the territorial people as his "little brown brothers" and wrote that they were:

"...a vast mass of ignorant, superstitious people...liars...nothing but grown up children...They need the training of fifty or a hundred years before they shall realize what Anglo-Saxon liberty is...the electoral franchise must be much limited, because the large majority will not, for a long time, be capable of intelligently exercising it."

While not politically correct by today's standards, the Governor of the Philippines who wrote those reports to Washington was in his day considered one of the most progressive minded U.S. government leaders in America. Whether or not ultimately motivated by "progressive" purposes as understood in the context of the times, the imperialism Taft practiced was tainted by the still-institutionalized racism and paternalistic presuppositions of cultural supremacy prevalent in America during his life and times.

Thus, in a keynote address at a 2014 symposium on the Insular Cases at Harvard Law School, Judge Juan R. Torruella, U.S. Federal Court of Appeals for the First Circuit, traced back to progressive imperialists at Harvard and Yale the "intellectual origins the Insular Cases." Specifically, Torruella cites an 1898 Harvard Law Review article urging Congress to deny "benefits of the Constitution" to the "ignorant and lawless brigands that infest Puerto Rico." The Supreme Court and Congress adopted precisely that policy in 1901, and in 2015 Congress still relies on Insular Cases to impose, in Torruella's words, "discriminatory rules...to keep millions in an inferior colonial condition."

As Governor in the Philippines the ambitious Taft embraced the Insular Cases as license for latitude to be both humanitarian and reign as supreme ruler. As a dedicated imperialist Taft insisted on a visible American program for modernization of roads, schools and hospitals. At the same time his government waged a brutal war against the native nationalists. Taft sought distraction from such dreadful business as war at splendid dinners of imperial grandeur, where terms were agreed for disbursement of American largesse to opportunistically pro-America elites in the Philippines.

When his mission as the first American ruler of the Philippines was over, Taft was rewarded for his robust progressive imperialism with nothing less than appointment to serve as President Theodore Roosevelt's Secretary of War.

The position most coveted by Taft, was that of Chief Justice on the U.S. Supreme Court. Since that job was not open, when Taft's tenure as Secretary of War ended, his ambitions turned to pursuit and attainment of a term as President of the United States.

After leaving the White House and becoming a professor at Yale Law School, the life long goal of William Howard Taft was fulfilled when he was, after all, appointed in 1921, as Chief Justice of the Supreme Court.

Taft knew that in 1901 the U.S. Supreme Court had excluded both the Philippines and Puerto Rico from the Northwest Ordinance tradition.

A year after he ascended to that position, Taft would have the opportunity to draw on his experience as an architect of progressive imperialism in the U.S. territories denied incorporation under the Insular Cases.

Thus, during the court's 1922 session, the new Chief Justice was able to assign himself the task of writing the court's decision in a case originating in Puerto Rico. As fate would have it, the court was being asked to determine the constitutional effect of a 1917 federal law in which Congress conferred U.S. citizenship in Puerto Rico.

Taft decidedly *did not* see the case of Balzac v. Puerto Rico as a repeat of the Alaska and Hawaii cases, but rather as an opportunity to reverse the effect of those two rulings without admitting it. Instead of following relevant precedent, Taft's purpose was to sustain the logic of imperial rule under the Insular Cases even *after* Congress conferred U.S. citizenship.

Thus, Taft was only too ready for the project and happily assured the rest of the court that he would write the opinion in the Puerto Rico citizenship case.

Taft was determined Puerto Rico would remain "unincorporated" even after U.S. citizenship was granted. However, by 1905 the U.S. Supreme Court had ruled that both Hawaii and Alaska had been incorporated based on conferral of U.S. citizenship at the time of annexation. Still, Taft engineered a ruling in 1922 treating the passage of time between annexation in 1900 and conferral of citizenship by Congress in 1917 as justification for denial of incorporation.

In a sense, the Balzac ruling means that once a territory populated by non-citizens is classified as unincorporated under the Insular Cases, conferral of U.S. citizenship at a later time has a constitutional meaning entirely different than if citizenship had been conferred at the time the U.S. acquired sovereignty over the territory.

Still, there is no plausible logic to the fabricated notion that the constitutional effect of citizenship depends on the timing of its conferral in relationship to the time of annexation.

In fact, conferral of citizenship in a territory previously inhabited by non-citizens objectively must have a constitutionally indistinguishable meaning and effect regardless of its relationship in time to acquisition of sovereignty.

Instead, after Balzac it would be the court that would decide if the Northwest Ordinance or the Insular Cases model would apply to U.S. citizen populated territories.

The admission of Louisiana, Alaska and Hawaii, arguably Florida, California and New Mexico as well, are still binding legal and political precedents that reveal Balzac's flawed reasoning.

In Balzac, Taft asserts without grounds that the courts cannot interpret the effect of conferring U.S. citizenship unless Congress explicitly states its' intent as to the effect of U.S. citizenship on the political status of a territory classified as unincorporated.

Taft's clear intention was to make sure Congress could never again act unilaterally to confer U.S. citizenship and thereby extend to a territory both the Constitution and the promise of eventual equal citizenship through statehood. Instead, after Balzac it would be the court that would decide if the Northwest Ordinance or the Insular Cases model would apply to U.S. citizen populated territories.

In his opinion Taft essentially proclaims by judicial edict that the status of a territory classified as unincorporated under the Insular Cases is not altered by a change in the citizenship status of the territorial population. *Making no bones about it, Taft, in his opinion for the court, invites anyone in Puerto Rico who wants rights under the Constitution to relocate to a State and thereby acquire equal civil and political rights!*

The meaning of this ruling is that Congress can confer U.S. citizenship without extending application of the Constitution to the population whose status has changed from that of non-citizens to the same citizenship as Americans in the fifty states. The implication is that conferral of citizenship is a consequence free activity and has no effect on the legal rights or political status of territorial people under federal territorial law and policy.

The practical effect is that Congress can extend citizenship without being required to determine the question of whether the territory will ever qualify for incorporation leading to statehood. At the same time, Balzac allows Congress to govern the territory indefinitely without adopting a policy leading to nationhood consistent with the right of independence.

This is a direct and material contradiction of the original Insular Cases doctrine in Downes v. Bidwell, which explicitly stated the ruling applied only to non-citizens populated territories, and only until Congress decided the issue of citizenship. More fundamentally, the Balzac doctrine is one of indefinite if not perpetual territorial status outside the U.S. Constitution for a U.S. citizen populated territory. As such, it is an open and flagrant assault on the anti-colonial principles of the Northwest Ordinance, which explicitly states that all forms of territory government under U.S. rule are "temporary," until

The implication is that conferral of citizenship is a consequence-free activity and has no effect on the legal rights or political status of territorial people under federal territorial law and policy.

The practical effect is that Congress can extend citizenship without being required to determine the question of whether the territory will ever qualify for incorporation leading to statehood.

★ ★ ★

This is a direct and material contradiction of the original Insular Cases doctrine applicable only temporarily in U.S. territories with non-citizen populations.

incorporation leads to statehood, as reiterated by the Supreme Court in 1957 (Reid v. Covert).

As such, the Balzac ruling as contrived by Taft separated U.S. national citizenship conferred by statute in the territories from the Constitution. The ruling creates the possibility of permanent territorial status with national citizenship, but without equal rights and duties under the Constitution that arise only from State citizenship.

As such, the Balzac ruling not only deviates from the anti-colonial values and traditions of the Northwest Ordinance, the court's decision in the case is defective in its logic and legal thesis.

In contrast to the Court's rigorously reasoned opinions in the Insular Cases, Taft's opinion in Balzac was intellectually shallow and paternalistic. Obviously deferring to the heavy-handed insistence of the Chief Justice the Court washed its hands of Puerto Rico's fate. It did so by unanimously signing off on the following intellectually flippant treatment in the ruling of the solemn act of conferring birthright citizenship in Puerto Rico:

"It became a yearning of the Puerto Ricans to be American citizens and this act [by Congress] gave them the boon...What additional rights did it give them? It enabled them to move into the continental United States...and enjoy every right of any other citizen."

This institutionalized a doctrine of inequality for which geographic relocation of citizens within the nation is the only remedy. Apparently still captive to the "white man's burden" myth so predominant among progressive imperialists when he was Governor in the Philippines, Taft sought foremost to protect the American people from admission of another state populated by an "alien race" into the Union.

Thus, in the Alaska and Hawaii cases, and historically in the case of Louisiana, the court had ruled that conferring citizenship required the judiciary to "infer" that citizenship meant incorporation and application of the Constitution.

Yet, Taft's opinion asserts that a determination of whether citizenship leads to incorporation must not be "left a matter of mere inference."

Similarly, writing the opinion lamentably adopted by the court in Balzac the imperious Taft admits,

"It is true that in the absence of other and countervailing evidence, a law of Congress or a provision in a treaty... declaring an intention to confer political and civil rights on the inhabitants of the new lands as American citizens, may be properly interpreted to mean an incorporation of it into the union, as in the case of...Alaska."

But in a stunningly disingenuous feint, instead of citing any countervailing evidence or presenting plausible distinctions between the Alaska and Puerto Rico cases, Taft lamely offers the following untenable excuse for the anomalous ruling:

"Alaska was a very different case from that of Puerto Rico. It was an enormous territory, very sparsely settled, and offering opportunity for immigration and settlement by American citizens. It was on the American continent and within easy reach of the then United States. It involved none of the difficulties which incorporation of the Philippines and Puerto Rico presents..."

It was true that Alaska geographically was larger than Puerto Rico, but that was also true of most states, including Hawaii when the Court ruled two years after the Alaska case that the islands were incorporated based on conferral of U.S. citizenship.

Taft argued Alaska's sparse population made it more attractive than Puerto Rico as a destination for settlers. Apparently he had never been in Alaska or Puerto Rico in February, which might have changed his perspective on why Alaska is so sparsely populated and Puerto Rico is not. Taft was correct that Alaska is appurtenant to the North American continent, but it was the first non-contiguous territory not reachable by land without leaving U.S. territory.

For Taft to compare the "difficulties" of incorporating Puerto Rico to the Philippines was overtly misleading. The Philippines was on the other side of the globe, as foreign as foreign gets. Puerto Rico was in America's backyard and within the zone of the Monroe Doctrine.

The U.S. had fought a costly, bloody and protracted war to defeat armed insurrection in the Philippines. In contrast, the independence movement in Puerto Rico was more comparable to independence movements in Vermont and Texas, and less violent than the anarchist and communist movements in the U.S. at the time Balzac was decided.

In 1916, the U.S. declared a policy denying citizenship or statehood for the Philippines. In 1917, Congress did the opposite and conferred U.S. citizenship in Puerto Rico and organized a territorial government without addressing status resolution. It had done the same in Alaska and Hawaii, determined by the Court to have been incorporated into the union based on conferral of citizenship.

Perhaps the inconsistency in results for Puerto Rico under Taft's logic explains why Associate Justice Oliver Wendell Holmes deferred to the Chief Justice's insistence on having his way, but simply "concurred in the result" without associating himself with the legal reasoning of the ruling.

Regrettably, the opinion represents an abuse of power for reasons of personal bias by Chief Justice Taft to which no member of the court should have submitted. But that was court politics run amuck and the non-meritorious content of the opinion is of little import. It was the result that Holmes and the other justices should never have embraced, because it was and remains one of the worst rulings the court has ever issued.

10

Restoring Northwest Ordinance Principles For Puerto Rico

The Northwest Ordinance was an enabling act for statehood. It was applicable to a region that eventually was divided into Ohio, Indiana, Illinois, and other territories which became States. It constituted a compact of assurance by Congress for U.S. citizens in the territories, defining the criteria for statehood.

Enabling acts in the Northwest Ordinance tradition include the following requirements for statehood:

★ *Geographic size and population as large as existing States*

★ *Republican form of government under a statehood constitution*

★ *Economic provisions and political transition to statehood*

Most territories became states under separate enabling acts consistent with Northwest Ordinance.

Separate enabling acts do not create irrevocable criteria for admission, preclude petitions, seeking different terms for admission, or restrict agreement by Congress and the territory to adjust terms of transition during the final stage of integration under admission act.

Puerto Rico already exceeds historical criteria for statehood and is far more integrated into the union today than most if not all 32 territories admitted under Northwest Ordinance model:

★ *Puerto Rico's population (3.6 million) is greater than that of twenty-two states, which does not include population of citizens from Puerto Rico living in fifty states (5 million).*

★ *U.S. citizenship at birth has been federal law in Puerto Rico for 98 years, soon a century of common citizenship with the rest of America.*

★ *Republican form of local government under a constitution ratified by the people and U.S. Congress has been in effect for 63 years.*

★ *The Constitution, laws and treaties of the United States have been supreme law of the land in territory for 114 years.*

★ *Puerto Rico voted for statehood by sixty-one percent in 2012, with more votes cast separately for statehood than for current status, which was rejected by fifty-four percent in separate up or down vote.*

★ *Government and private studies show a private sector encumbered by limitations of current status, but predict stability, and sustainable growth under statehood, enabling Puerto Rico to pay its way in the Union.*

★ *Puerto Rico is three times the size of Rhode Island, larger than Delaware, with the same combined land and waters as Connecticut, and Puerto Rico's coastal marine zone equals Georgia's, but is larger than that of South Carolina's, New Jersey, Pennsylvania.*

★ *Federal court rulings have recognized virtual incorporation of the territory, citing Congressional confirmation of federal judges in Puerto Rico under U.S. Const. Art. III, appointment of U.S. citizens from Puerto Rico as U.S. Ambassadors under Art. II, and noting U.S. citizens from Puerto Rico in the U.S. armed forces are appointed to rank of General and Admiral like U.S. citizens from States, not to mention that a U.S. citizen from the territory now serves on the U.S. Supreme Court.*

Congress should treat U.S. citizens of Puerto Rico like other statehood eligible territories throughout history, including adoption of an enabling act defining conditions for attaining statehood, followed by an admissions act on terms acceptable to Congress.[9] In that context, a vote to reaffirm the 2012 vote

9 Self-determination for territories must, of course, be differentiated from democratization of the District of Columbia, another federal reservation not within any State, where the Twenty-third Amendment conferred the right State citizens have to vote for President. Like federal relations with the Native Americans of the "Indian Nations," the federal city in our nation's capital is not governed under the same Constitutional text or body of law as the territories. Unlike the thirty two historical precedents for incorporation and admission of territories, there is no historical precedent for permanently vesting further rights of State citizenship in D.C. other than by another constitutional amendment.

Thus, for Washington D.C. the option of statehood or a constitutional amendment to secure Congressional representation may or may not prove attainable. If not, it would be consistent with the principle of self-determination under U.N. human rights conventions to which the U.S. is a party to offer our fellow Americans in those parts of the federal city not dedicated to national government use the option of reintegration (retrocession) into Maryland. Since those areas originally were ceded from Maryland, Congress and the state legislature would have to approve retrocession. Presumably that would be considered only if citizens of D.C. voted to end the current provisional regime of "home rule" established under federal law and overseen by Congress.

for statehood will be a celebration of self-determination for our nation, also showing the world that government by consent of the governed is still the driving moral force that makes the USA the land of the free.

Afterword
The Prospect Now Before Us...

Today the island territory of Puerto Rico presents Congress with the same question it has faced on thirty-two previous occasions when territories became States:

How will the U.S. govern permanently U.S. citizens residing in a federal territorial possession that is under U.S. sovereignty within our national borders, and do so in a manner that upholds the U.S. Constitution?

In all previous thirty-two cases the only answer that could be given was to establish a mechanism to make it possible for the U.S. citizens of each such territory otherwise eligible under historical criteria to make an orderly transition to admission as a State of the Union. In each case admission was on such terms as were consented to by Congress and the U.S. citizens of the territory concerned.

The reason that was the only answer that could be given is that statehood is the only political status through which U.S. citizens can acquire and secure permanently equal rights and duties of national and State citizenship under the Constitution. For constitutionally, any form of territorial government and territorial status itself is purely temporary.

It is within the constitutional authority and responsibility of Congress to admit Puerto Rico as a State of the Union, based on nearly a century of U.S. national citizenship.

Five decades of experimentation with a failed theory of autonomic territorial self-government as an implausible

> For constitutionally, any form of territorial government and territorial status itself is purely temporary.

substitute for statehood or nationhood has offered no path to successful status resolution. History calls for the U.S. citizens of the territory to have a truly free choice to inhabit rather than flee from their cultural homeland.

That must include a choice to live in Puerto Rico with the rights of national citizenship that are secured only when one lives in a State of the Union. For only then will our fellow Americans in Puerto Rico no longer be "Citizens Without A State."

A Statehood Primer

History of Statehood: Lessons for Puerto Rico

The history of statehood in America includes the emergence of the original thirteen self-declared "States" that asserted sovereignty in defiance of British colonial rule, joined the Continental Congress, and ratified the Articles of Confederation in 1781.

After the thirteen confederated States formed a more perfect union under the U.S. Constitution in 1789, thirty-two federal territories, four regions partitioned from existing States, and one independent Republic would be admitted as new States.

Today, each State's story holds lessons for the U.S. citizens of Puerto Rico, who face many of the same challenges overcome by the thirty-two territories that became States.

The First Thirteen States

Governing outlying territories in America was always challenging and often contentious. In 1763, the King of England reclaimed unsettled western lands promised to the colonies. The Declaration of Independence cited as unjust the Crown's interference with settlement of new lands by citizens and immigrants.

Disputes among the original thirteen States and with the federal government over claims in western territories delayed ratification of the Articles of Confederation.

Under the Articles of Confederation in 1787 the first thirteen States adopted the Northwest Ordinance, providing for "temporary" territorial governments until a duly constituted citizenry applied for statehood. The first U.S. Congress assembled under the Constitution in 1789, and adopted the Northwest Ordinance of 1787 as federal statutory law.

The original ordinance of 1787 proclaimed itself a *"compact...unalterable, unless by common consent."* However, after 1789, only the Constitution was permanent law, unalterable unless amended under Article V. *All* statutory law was now amendable, and one Congress could not by statute bind a later Congress. Consent of the governed was now given through federal voting rights of citizens in the States.

Re-enacted by Congress as an *Article I* statute in 1789, the Northwest Ordinance could be amended or repealed the same as any federal law. Accordingly, Congress organized territories under the ordinance and often altered its terms without consent of territorial governments.

THE LESSON FOR PUERTO RICO:

In 1950, the terms "...in the nature of a compact..." and "...recognizing the principle of government by consent" appeared in a federal territorial organizing statute ("organic act") allowing joint local and Congressional ratification of a territorial constitution in Puerto Rico. Use of those terms didn't define or change the territory's political status or make the territorial government constitutionally permanent.

Rather, federal policy emanating from the Northwest Ordinance continued—thus allowing local civil government based on self-determination—but subject to federal law. Constitutionally, Congress can amend or repeal statutory law to alter Puerto Rico's current form of territorial government, and otherwise determine its political status.

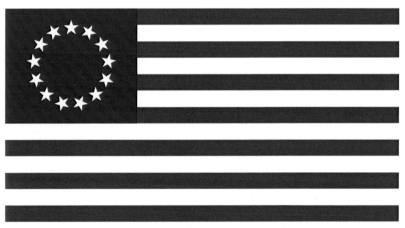

13 Stars "Betsy Ross"

Vermont
1791 ★ The 14th State

Vermont was not a territory, but was formed instead from the territory of New York. The Constitution (Art. IV Sec. 3) required permission of the State Legislature, but initially New York and Congress were unresponsive to Vermont's petitions.

Boldly reasserting a colonial-era claim of independence, Vermont's leaders shrewdly began exploring recognition of its sovereignty by England. After 15 years of brinkmanship by Vermont, Congress and New York accepted the will of Vermont's people to achieve liberty and equality through statehood rather than independence.

LESSON FOR PUERTO RICO:

Like Vermont, Puerto Rico can seek independence, with or without a treaty of free association with the United States. However, any form of separate soverign nationhood will end U.S. citizenship and the island's progress toward permanent Union with full citizenship equality through statehood.

Kentucky
1792 ★ The 15th State

When Kentucky petitioned for separation from Virginia and eventual statehood, the Virginia legislature demanded, in essence, that Kentucky *pay* for the right to become a State. So, under both the Articles of Confederation and later the U.S. Constitution, the region known as Western Virginia used flirtations with foreign powers to give the central government and Virginia new incentives to admit Kentucky as a State.

Britain wanted an ally and Spain wanted to limit expansion of the Americans into the Southwest region it claimed. The risk to the U.S. was just credible enough that the central government supported partition and Virginia finally offered terms Kentucky could accept, leading to admission.

LESSON FOR PUERTO RICO:

Short term fiscal pressures and demands recede when Congress knows the territory will accept no outcome except statehood.

15 Stars & 15 Stripes
"Star-Spangled Banner"

Tennessee
1796 ★ The 16th State

Tennessee was the first "territory" governed under the Territory Clause of the Constitution, after it was partitioned from North Carolina under the Articles of Confederation. It was organized under federal law based on the Northwest Ordinance model that applied in greater Ohio. Kentucky, less patient than Ohio, famously *adopted* a constitution, *declared* statehood and sent an elected Congressional delegation to Congress.

It worked! Tennessee was admitted as a State, but only after new elections for its Congressional delegation, since under Article I of the Constitution only citizens of a State (not a territory) can elect full voting members of Congress.

Six other territories, Michigan (1837), Iowa (1846), California (1850), Oregon (1859), Kansas (1861), and Alaska (1959) adopted a variation of the Tennessee Plan to successfully force admission to statehood.

LESSON FOR PUERTO RICO:

The "Tennessee Plan" can backfire (e.g. Missouri and New Mexico) if the partisan climate in Washington is not right. Puerto Rico needs to consider each Tennessee Plan case study and adapt strategy to deal with both the foreseeable and unexpected. Admission is a political question, so judicial classification as an "unincorporated" territory is secondary to what Puerto Rico has in common with all territories that became States: U.S. citizenship.

Ohio
1803 ★ The 17th State

Ohio was the original territory where the Northwest Ordinance of 1787 applied. After the Constitution took effect in 1789, the Northwest Territory was divided up into Ohio and the greater Indiana Territory. Ohio became the lead territory seeking admission as a State, but territorial government leaders actually opposed statehood to stay in power. The pro-statehood movement finally out-maneuvered the territorial regime in Congress, and Ohio became a State in 1803.

LESSON FOR PUERTO RICO:

Territorial government resistance to statehood is a typical pattern in many territories—including Puerto Rico today. In modern era territories like Alaska and Hawaii, federal and local territorial leaders and special interests delayed statehood to exploit the political and economic asymmetries of territorial status for power, profit, or both.

History shows the greatest good for the greatest number of people is realized through the far more level playing field and sustainable prosperity experienced by every territory that has become a State.

Louisiana
1812 ★ The 18th State

The State of Louisiana was formed out of the vast un-surveyed lands ceded to the U.S. by France in the "Louisiana Purchase" of 1803. Economic underdevelopment and lack of social integration with the rest of the nation complicated incorporation of the territory. French and Spanish were the languages of society, politics, business and law, and admission of another slave State (with a free mulatto class) was sharply divisive.

Yet, failure to secure effective sovereign control invited foreign power encroachment, and Congress had already granted citizenship, triggering the Northwest Ordinance model of incorporation. Thus, even during our second war with Britain in 1812, Louisiana was the first of several States admitted from the region ceded by France.

LESSON FOR PUERTO RICO:

Puerto Rico today is far more integrated into the nation's economy and the life of the nation generally than Louisiana, or most territories that became States.

In 1812, Congress realized cultural and economic challenges made denial of statehood the only thing more problematic than admission. The anti-statehood party in Puerto Rico wants Congress to see continued territory status as a way to avoid statehood. As a result, the pro-statehood movement now must remind Congress that once citizenship is granted a court-invented unincorporated territory status *becomes* the problem, not a way to avoid it, and historically statehood is the only *proven* solution.

Indiana
1816 ★ The 19th State

After partition from Ohio, the vast Indiana Territory would itself be divided to create a new territory named Illinois.

The Northwest Ordinance contained an anti-slavery clause codified by Congress in Indiana's organic act. Slave owners who proposed lifting the ban had an ally in the Governor of the territory, but facing strong opposition a compromise was reached limiting slavery to existing levels.

Having compromised on slavery, Indiana proposed and won federal concessions in its admissions act, including five percent of the proceeds from federal land sales in the territory to put State finances on a sound footing, as well as generous grants of lands for public schools and the State seat of government.

LESSON FOR PUERTO RICO:

A territory may have to compromise on national issues to win statehood and gain representation in Congress, where issues impacting the future of the citizens will be decided.

Mississippi
1817 ★ The 20TH State

After the State of Georgia abandoned colonial era claims to the lands that became Mississippi, American settlers began an irreversible incursion into Spanish held areas west of Florida that would become Mississippi and Alabama. Mississippi was admitted in 1817, despite entrenched opposition from anti-slavery forces due to its legalized slave trade.

LESSON FOR PUERTO RICO:

Divisive national issues are just that, national issues. Territories should not be singled out and denied statehood based on national issues that need to be resolved nationally. Whatever solution is found for the nation will apply in the new State. Congress can apply any federal law to a territory, only through statehood are local interests protected by equal representation in Congress.

20 Stars

Illinois
1818 ★ The 21st State

Using the anti-colonial mechanisms of the Northwest Ordinance, the original Northwest Territory from which Ohio and Indiana were formed was then divided to form Illinois and later Wisconsin, as well as parts of Michigan and Minnesota.

After the admission of Indiana as a State in 1812, Illinois was next.

The original Northwest Ordinance specified a population of sixty-thousand as sufficient for admission. Yet, by 1817, when Illinois petitioned for statehood, the average population of the first twenty States was thirty-five thousand. Due to pressure from several southern and northern territories seeking admission, Congress fast-tracked Illinois by altering the Northwest Ordinance to lower the population threshold to forty-thousand.

Still, the most recent census preliminarily indicated a population of thirty-three thousand. "Supplemental" census-taking conveniently boosted the headcount to forty-thousand, two hundred and fifty-eight. Statehood was won!

LESSON FOR PUERTO RICO:

Congress can undo whatever it has done by statute. If a statute could be made permanent that, in effect, would amend the Constitution by taking *away* the power of Congress to change the law. Consent is not required for Congress to change a statutory or organic act provision that is "in the nature of a compact" but still subject to the supremacy of federal law. The issue for Puerto Rico is whether it will be represented in Congress when it acts.

Alabama
1819 ★ The 22nd State

In 1817, slaves constituted almost a third of the population of Alabama, formerly eastern Mississippi. Not surprisingly the economy was booming.

During the previous decade, brutal Indian wars devastated the region's native tribes. That epic clash of cultures over slavery and/or Indian exile played out in Alabama as it did in most territories.

Despite those limiting factors, the political process of the territory wasn't impeded. In early 1819, a statehood constitution was ratified by a convention comprising representatives of the territory's twenty-two counties.

Instead of submitting the constitution for ratification by the voters, the new constitution was simply sent to Congress, which then fast-tracked a statehood act.

Wasting no time on a political status referendum, elections were held under the new constitution so the new statehood government could be formed, and before the year ended Alabama was a State.

LESSON FOR PUERTO RICO:

Admission to statehood is a *political* action by Congress. Several territories were admitted without a referendum, and the transition procedures under local and federal law varies widely.

Having adopted a republican form of government under a territorial constitution sixty-five years *before* this writing, and having had a fully sufficient act of self-determination approving statehood in 2012, the government of Puerto Rico has both *the legal and moral authority* to seek admission on terms acceptable to Congress.

A referendum on the terms of admission certainly would be expected, given modern era principles of self-determination, but that's still more of a *political* than legal question.

22 Stars

Maine
1820 ★ The 23rd State

Maine's separate statehood movement began under the Articles of Confederation, but didn't succeed until Congress and the State of Massachusetts finally agreed on partition—31 years after the Constitution took effect!

Being governed from Boston and paying taxes without perceived benefits was unpopular in the Northwest, a region that voted *seventy-one percent* for separate statehood in 1819, and then ratified a statehood constitution by *ninety-two* percent.

The consent of Massachusetts required Congress to act on admission by a date certain, but as the deadline neared, admission of Maine was held hostage when Missouri sought to follow recently admitted Alabama as another new slave State. Even with the admission of Maine that would tip the balance between free and slave States to favor the latter.

The compromise reached allowed Maine to be admitted as a free State, Missouri as slave, but it prohibited expansion of slavery into any other territory or State in the northern tier of the country other than Missouri. The "Missouri Compromise" would later be declared unconstitutional, but in 1820, it enabled Maine to become a State.

LESSON FOR PUERTO RICO:

Statehood can and probably will be linked to national issues over which the territory has little or no control, and that may have little or nothing to do with the territory itself. Pro-statehood forces play a vital role in the deliberations of Congress in these critical moments when political pressure is high and time is running out.

Missouri
1821 ★ The 24th State

By 1816, after a hard-luck territorial history, statehood for Missouri seemed promising, but it blew up into a national confrontation in 1817, after petitioning Congress for admission as a slave State.

After two full years of vociferous north-south debate in Congress, the "Missouri Compromise" was reached. The trade-off was admission of Maine as a free state, with Missouri designated as the last slave State in the northermost tier of States formed from the territories acquired in the Louisiana Purchase.

But even then admission stalled because Missouri's constitution allowed exclusion of freed "negroes or mulattoes" from other states. It took what we'll call a "Second Missouri Compromise" denying federal assent to exclusion of "emancipated slaves" before Missouri's admission a year after Maine's.

That preserved federal power to nullify any exercise of the exclusionary power by Missouri, one more example of compromises that would delay but not avert the Civil War.

LESSON FOR PUERTO RICO:

In 1952, Congress amended the Puerto Rico territorial constitution to *preclude* mischief arising from ambiguity about supremacy of federal law. Mischief was made by "antonomists" anyway, but that merely delayed the territory's progress toward statehood. Territories may seek special rights, and new States may win transitional concessions, but the *genius* of our nation is *equal* rights. It is statehood on equal footing with every State that leads to sustainable and permanent liberty and prosperity for the United States.

Arkansas
1836 ★ The 25th State

Separated from Missouri before it became a State, it was not until 1835, that the Arkansas Territory's delegate in Congress, the territorial legislature and the public took a focused interest in seeking admission to the Union.

Michigan was pursing a "Tennessee Plan" strategy, declaring itself a de facto state. As a slave-trade territory, adoption of a statehood constitution and pursuit of admission by Arkansas in tandem with Michigan would improve odds for both territories.

Arkansas' Governor, apparently comfortable with the status quo, asked the U.S. Attorney General to opine on whether, as a creation of Congress, a territory could adopt a statehood constitution without authorization *by* Congress. Legal issues impeded political change, until a referendum in which sixty-eight percent voted for statehood.

The pro-statehood alliance outmaneuvered the anti-slavery caucus. Arkansas beat Michigan in the race to be a State.

LESSON FOR PUERTO RICO:

Vested interests deriving power, wealth or both from territorial status will use legal tactics to prevent territorial status resolution. In the end, the pro-statehood majority must stand up and seize the rights of equality, instead of quibbling and dithering over legal and ideological abstractions anti-statehood interests propound to confuse issues and perpetuate the status quo.

Michigan
1837 ★ The 26th State

By 1832, Michigan had resisted merger with other Northwest Ordinance territories, endured the War of 1812, and chronic Indian conflicts. When the Erie Canal opened Lake Michigan to steamship navigation in 1825, a robust economic recovery followed, and statehood seemed within reach.

In 1832, a referendum majority favored statehood. However, boundary disputes impeded progress in Congress.

A constitutional convention was called. Alarmingly, Michigan and Ohio troops were mobilized in the event of an open conflict over borders declared by Michigan's constitutional convention. The constitution won approval by eighty-two percent of voters in 1835—the Governor declared Michigan a State, and congressional elections were held.

President Jackson believed Michigan would help elect Van Buren in 1836's presidential race, so he supported admission. Congress agreed, the boundaries were re-drawn.

LESSON FOR PUERTO RICO:

The *citizens* give consent to the rights and duties of statehood for the territory, the *Congress* gives consent for the States of the Union.

Florida
1845 ★ The 27th State

Spain eventually would lose Oregon, Mexico, Puerto Rico and Cuba, but in 1821, it lost Florida. The treaty of cession recognized U.S. citizenship, resulting in incorporation.

In 1837, statehood won a referendum by sixty-three percent. Anti-statehood interests challenged the results because voters in some regional precincts cast ballots for candidates on the ballot but left the question on statehood blank.

Despite efforts to divide the territory, a statehood constitution was approved in 1839. It languished until a pro-statehood delegate was elected to Congress in 1841.

Admission of Florida as a slave State was approved by Congress along with Iowa as a free state.

Like other coastal states, disputes arose about federal and state jurisdiction over submerged land and marine zones.

LESSON FOR PUERTO RICO:

As with calls to single out Puerto Rico to require a super-majority for admission, counting blank ballots is anti-democratic.

Puerto Rico should secure State rights out to three leagues, and economic rights beyond in the statehood admission act based on settled precedent, not in the courts *after* admission.

Texas
1845 ★ The 28th State

Texas in 1835, was a neglected province of Mexico's Coahuila State, then an independent nation, until ninety-seven precent of voters approved annexation under a statehood constitution. By 1845, Texas was a State.

Texas seceded in the Civil War, but the Supreme Court ruled Texas did not *cease* being a State. That 1868 ruling confirms that the States were *sovereign* and joined the Union by both *consent of each State admitted*, and *consent of the Union* to admission of each State.

That means statehood is a *permanent* political status that cannot be changed *without consent by the State and the Union*.

LESSON FOR PUERTO RICO:

Statehood is the *only* status defined by the U.S. Constitution allowing U.S. citizens in Puerto Rico to *guarantee* their grandchildren will be U.S. citizens living in the United States of America.

Puerto Rico's anti-statehood party *claims* a local constitution ended territorial status and that so-called *"commonwealth"* is a *"constitutional relationship"* between the local and federal governments.

Rather, it's a *statutory* relationship between *federal and territorial* authorities. All territorial governments remain constitutionally *"temporary,"* as originally defined in the Northwest Ordinance.

The 1868 federal court ruling on Texas statehood defined it as "a political community of free citizens" consenting to "indissoluble...perpetual union." That meant even secession from the Union in the Civil War did not end statehood as the constitutionally recognized status of Texas.

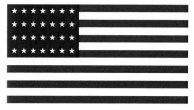

28 Stars

Iowa
1846 ★ The 29th State

A "remnant" of the Louisiana Purchase regions, Iowa was appended to, then cast off—first by Missouri, then Wisconsin. By 1840, it overcame formidable hurdles as a frontier territory and petitioned for statehood.

Iowa was a slave-free territory approved for admission in tandem with pro-slavery Florida in 1945. However, Congress tampered with boundary lines in the statehood constitution, so Iowa *twice* voted down revised constitutions, adopting a modified Tennessee plan, electing a Congressional delegation. Concessions were made, statehood was proclaimed, Tennessee Plan representatives were seated in Congress.

LESSONS FOR PUERTO RICO:

Puerto Rico needs to reject any notion U.S. citizenship in Puerto Rico is less important than U.S. citizenship in an incorporated territory.

The fact that Congress has not come to grips with the irrationality of 1922's Balzac case applying unincorporated territory doctrine after citizenship was granted is Congress' problem, not Puerto Rico's.

Rico is the last large territory with a U.S. citizen population not admitted to statehood, despite the fact that it *exceeds* compliance with all criteria for statehood applied to those thirty-two territories that became states.

Wisconsin
1848 ★ The 30th State

Before mineral discoveries triggered migration of U.S. citizens into California and Alaska, by 1820, lead-mining accelerated migration that hastened Wisconsin's incorporation into the Union. After years of Indian wars, treaties for removal of tribes and booming land speculation prompted a Northwest Ordinance organic act in 1836.

Wisconsin's citizens did not accept boundaries drawn by Congress for Illinois and Michigan, and protested by rejecting statehood in 1839, 1842, and 1844. Just twenty-two percent voted to seek admission in 1844. Finally statehood was approved in 1846, but voters then *rejected* a state-of-the-art statehood constitution in 1846.

A second constitutional convention wrote a new proposed constitution approved in 1847, and Wisconsin was admitted in 1848.

No wonder Wisconsin leaders thought better of a Tennessee Plan strategy putting up a statehood slate to elect a Congressional delegation. The risk was too high that voters would reject *all* the candidates, or even the *idea* of having a delegation!

LESSONS FOR PUERTO RICO:

A history of inconclusive status votes becomes virtually irrelevant once a majority vote for statehood. The territorial regime and special interests benefitting from the status quo may obstruct the political process, but the pro-statehood forces always prevail in the end. Pro-statehood forces must make the case that statehood will best serve the interests not just of the territory but also the U.S. as a nation.

California
1850 ★ The 31st State

California was ceded by Mexico to the U.S. as war booty, declared a "republic," then placed under U.S. military government.

There was no gradual incorporation under federal territorial organizing law conferring citizenship on its mostly foreign population. California became a state when 100,000 U.S. citizens from every State and territory invaded in 1848, to search for gold.

By 1849, a populist statehood movement compelled the military governor to call a constitutional convention. Two months later voters approved a State constitution by ninety-five percent, at the same time electing two members to serve in the House. The State legislature convened and elected two U.S. Senators.

In Washington the California delegation proved disciplined and articulate. By early 1850, most in Congress, along with President Tyler, were sold.

Calls for partition into a slave State to the south and free state in the north were rejected. The citizens had ratified a constitution for *one* free State, and a package of compromises on slavery policy in other territories cleared the way for admission.

LESSONS FOR PUERTO RICO:

California was an unorganized territory with a majority non-citizen population. *A year later it was a free State with a majority U.S. citizen population.* Three and a half million U.S. citizens in Puerto Rico can do the same.

Minnesota
1858 ★ The 32nd State

Minnesota was not part of the Northwest Territory or the lands acquired in the Louisiana Purchase. That did not exempt Minnesota from chronic border disputes typical of the land crunch along the northern borderline.

After Wisconsin became a State in 1848, a delegate was elected to represent a small "leftover" territory orphaned by Wisconsin, which later merged with Minnesota.

A raucous political battle between two competing constitutional conventions ended when a new draft constitution was approved in 1858. Notably, it imposed a deadline purporting to trigger independence if Congress failed to act that year, but Congress and the President acted before that threat was put to the test.

By 1858 the Missouri Compromise had been declared unconstitutional by the U.S. Supreme Court in the Dred Scott case of 1857. Yet, as the nation spiraled toward cataclysm, there was no great battle over slavery in far-flung Minnesota.

LESSONS FOR PUERTO RICO:

There is no right to statehood, but once citizenship is granted independence should not be the only alternative to territorial status.

Vermont, Kentucky and Texas flirted with England, and perhaps China would covet the closed U.S. nuclear submarine base in Puerto Rico! But 2012's majority vote for statehood trumps political stunts as the moral and political predicate for Congress to enable Puerto Rico to seek statehood.

Oregon
1859 ★ The 33rd State

Spain, Britain and the U.S. had competing claims to the vast Oregon region, but treaties memorializing "agreement to disagree" over claims allowed all interests to thrive.

In 1846, the U.S. and England agreed on the Canadian border and the Oregon Territory became American. A provisional government was formed to fight Indians, and in 1848, an organic act was followed by petitions to end "anti-republican" territorial government.

Congress partitioned Oregon to create Washington, and eventually Idaho, Wyoming and Montana. Meanwhile, voters in Oregon voted down statehood in 1854, 1855, and 1856. In 1857, voters finally approved a convention for a statehood constitution. State officials were elected before admission, so territorial and State government existed at the same time.

That modified Tennessee Plan maneuver was resolved when Congress admitted Oregon as a State in 1859.

LESSONS FOR PUERTO RICO:

Puerto Rico's constitution will suffice for admission. As Congress adopts an admission act, a Congressional delegation can be elected and wait to be seated when statehood is achieved.

Kansas
1861 ★ The 34th State

As partition of Kansas from Nebraska neared, the Missouri Compromise was breaking down. Congress appeased the south with stronger fugitive slave laws, and pro-slavery leaders advocated territorial autonomy on slavery.

Meanwhile, anti-slavery forces in several free states engineered state laws giving fugitive slaves legal protection, invoking "state rights" under the 10th Amendment.

The Kansas-Nebraska Act of 1854, emboldened both sides in the escalating fight over slavery in Kansas. An invasion by increasingly militant abolitionists and pro-slavery migrants triggered a brutal struggle to control the slavery issue.

Between 1855 and 1861, the territorial government was rendered illegitimate by pro-slavery usurpation and adoption of a free-state constitution led to violent civil strife more typical of civil war. A competing pro-slavery constitution was rejected by voters, and a second free-state constitution won a subsequent vote.

Aghast by the mayhem and the prospect of it spreading, Washington hastened to admit Kansas as a free State.

LESSONS FOR PUERTO RICO:

Territorial regimes can fail, particularly if progress toward statehood is in a state of arrest. In Puerto Rico anti-statehood leaders within the territorial regime cling to discredited claims a 1952 vote approving a local constitution made the territory constitutionally sovereign. Yet, a 2012 democratic act of self-determination in favor of statehood is ignored.

The small independence party in Puerto Rico even repudiates democratic majority rule unless it favors independence.

Meanwhile, anti-statehood leaders blame Washington for failure by the institutions of local self-government to manage the economy competently. How much worse does it have to get for Congress to end a century of abdication and exercise its power to make Puerto Rico a nation or a state, based on informed self-determination?

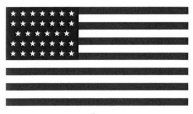

34 Stars

West Virginia
1863 ★ The 35th State

Voting against secession in 1861, the western counties of Virginia assembled regional conventions that boldly defied secessionist threats by endorsing loyalty to the Union. A separate State constitution was proposed by the provisional government.

Opponents of separate statehood convinced the U.S. Attorney General to advise Lincoln the provisional government lacked power to give State consent to partition. Lincoln ignored the political maneuver and shrewdly chose to recognize acts of the provisional government based on its loyalty to the Union.

Congress conditioned admission on amendment of the proposed statehood constitution to end slavery, that condition was met, and West Virginia became a State of the Union in its hour of greatest peril.

LESSONS FOR PUERTO RICO:

The U.S. citizens of Puerto Rico withdrew consent to territorial status by a 54% majority in the 2012 vote. Congressional action to create the mechanism for self-determination on a non-territorial status is the only way to restore government by consent for 3.5 million U.S. citizens.

Congress can sponsor votes to confirm 2012's 61% vote for statehood as a new status, or other mechanisms for self-determination under federal and local law, but it must act or abdicate its authority under the Constitution.

Nevada
1864 ★ The 36th State

The treaty of Guadalupe Hidalgo in 1848 ceded to the U.S. all or part of California, Nevada, Utah, Colorado, Arizona and New Mexico. Nevada was partitioned from the Territory of Utah after the seismic demographic shifts caused by the Gold Rush during the 1850s, which dislodged the region around Carson City from effective political control of territorial authorities in Salt Lake City, as well as Sacramento.

In 1861, Congress passed a territorial organic act and an accelerated Northwest Ordinance incorporation scenario ensued. By 1863, a strong majority voted to hold a convention to draft a statehood constitution.

However, mining interests opposed higher taxes anticipated with statehood, and officials enjoying job security in the territorial regime resisted any change of status. These special interests mounted a successful campaign to defeat ratification of the statehood constitution.

Pro-statehood leaders came back in 1864, with support from President Lincoln, who needed one more free State to approve an amendment to the U.S. Constitution ending slavery. A second convention adopted the first constitution, with revisions that excluded the mining industry from State taxation.

LESSONS FOR PUERTO RICO:

The very same political players and special interests that prevent admission in one session of Congress can become the strongest allies in the next session. That is, if their interests are accommodated or more powerful interests can be enlisted to defeat prior opposition.

Nebraska
1867 ★ The 37th State

The admission of California as a free state had been made possible by the "Compromise Measures of 1850," which embraced territorial autonomy so each territory could exercise "home rule" on slavery.

The territorial organic act of 1854 gave Nebraska autonomy but the citizens were conversant enough in the history of the Northwest Ordinance to know territorial government was temporary and eventually must culminate in statehood.

Enacted in 1859, a territorial law to allow a statehood constitution was defeated by voters. In an 1860 vote, only forty-seven percent approved statehood. In 1862, Congress approved a statehood-enabling act for Nebraska, but statehood opponents were elected as delegates to a convention and adjourned without action.

Two convention initiatives having failed, the territorial legislature acted without a federal enabling act and drafted a statehood constitution approved by voters in 1866. A territorial and statehood government coexisted until Congress authorized admission to statehood, subject to limitation of racial discrimination by the State to Indians who don't pay taxes.

LESSONS FOR PUERTO RICO:

Congress can exercise its power under the Territorial Clause in the U.S. Constitution to grant permissive statutory autonomy to a territory, but that does not define a constitutional status binding on a future Congress. Congress can nullify any federal law defining local powers, and any internal territorial law is void to the extent of incompatibility with federal law.

Colorado
1876 ★ The 38th State

The Mexican cession of 1848 enlarged the territory acquired in the Louisiana Purchase that became Colorado. Pioneers created provisional "home rule," but in the only direct political status vote, statehood received only forty-five percent. Instead, elected leaders petitioned Congress to become a territory under an organic act.

In 1861, an organic act was passed in Congress, and a statehood-enabling act was passed in 1864. In a now familiar pattern, the first statehood constitution was rejected in 1864, re-written in a four-day convention and approved in 1865.

With the end of the Civil War relations with the President were so bad that two new statehood-enabling bills passed by Congress were vetoed. Amidst readmission of rebel States and Reconstruction, Colorado was finally admitted in 1876.

LESSONS FOR PUERTO RICO:

Under the Constitution the government is not the source of rights, but rather citizens are the source of government powers. Dependency on the very territorial status that denies citizenship rights makes change uncertain. Territorial voters are more easily persuaded to oppose change than citizens in the States.

Citizens in Colorado failed to convince Congress that they were ready for statehood, and missed more than one window of opportunity due to internal political squabbling. An old story, best not repeated by Puerto Rico now that her citizens have spoken.

North & South Dakota
1889 ★ The 39th State
1889 ★ The 40th State

The Dakota Territory had been part of the greater Nebraska Territory when classified by law as the "Unorganized Territory." That meant no organic act had been adopted by Congress.

A federal organic act became law in 1861, but didn't create order. Washington couldn't unite farmers in the south with the wheat growers in the north, or the mining region of the Black Hills in the west. Each had ties to different markets in the east, and no use for one another.

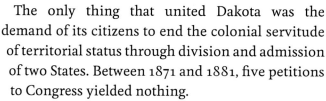

The only thing that united Dakota was the demand of its citizens to end the colonial servitude of territorial status through division and admission of two States. Between 1871 and 1881, five petitions to Congress yielded nothing.

In 1883, the south and then north held competing conventions, the south approved a constitution, and did it again in 1885, while a delegation of hundreds from the territory went to Washington demanding division and statehood.

Congress finally passed the 1889 Omnibus Bill enabling Montana, Washington and two Dakotas to hold conventions and votes to approve constitutions on terms prescribed by Congress.

LESSONS FOR PUERTO RICO:

Every minute spent talking about internal politics under the territorial regime is a minute wasted talking about how to persuade national political parties playing musical chairs in Washington that statehood is the only acceptable outcome, and thus inevitable.

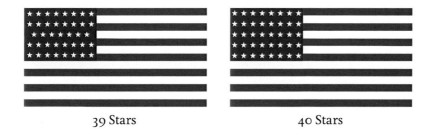

39 Stars   40 Stars

Montana
1889 ★ The 41st State

Most of Montana was a Louisiana Purchase territory that pioneers passed through on the way to somewhere else. Then in 1862, a small gold rush brought settlers, who created the first semblance of government by establishing offices to stake claims and record property title.

In 1864, Congress passed an organic act for the Territory of Montana. The first draft of a statehood constitution was adopted by a convention in 1866, but disappeared and was never found. The territorial legislature periodically adopted resolutions asking Congress to adopt a statehood-enabling act, but these were largely ignored.

The appointed territorial Governor from Washington was popular and successful. So it was not until 1888, that the territorial legislature called a convention and voters approved a statehood constitution.

There was consensus for statehood in the territory rather than partisan division, nevertheless Montana's petition for admission was linked to each national party's strategy for majority control of Congress. The impasse was broken by the 1889 Omnibus Bill, enabling statehood for Montana, Washington, and the Dakotas.

LESSONS FOR PUERTO RICO:

The Montana story reminds Puerto Rico that the sooner it stops wasting time talking about "autonomy" and independence, and changes the narrative based on self-determination for statehood, the better.

Even when statehood is the only democratic solution, petty partisan politics can delay admission by years.

Washington
1889 ★ The 42nd State

Citizens in the Territory of Washington were wary of statehood, until the anti-federal majority was swallowed-up by a population increase from 1853 to 1870. By 1878 the voters of Washington approved a statehood constitution, but Congress instead enacted a regional mechanism for admission of Washington, Dakota and Montana.

Oregon had become a State in 1859, and by 1889 Congress wanted the other Pacific Northwest territories to follow. A federal "Omnibus Bill" for those territories to hold statehood conventions was enacted, requiring revision of proposed constitutions until voter approval was achieved.

The Omnibus Bill worked. All four territories were admitted as states in 1889.

LESSONS FOR PUERTO RICO:

A majority of voters in Washington rejected statehood on general election ballots in 1869, and 1871. In both votes less than half of those casting ballots to elect local officials responded to the statehood question. Imagine if pro-statehood leaders had declared that statehood won by counting ballots left blank on the statehood question as votes for *statehood*!

That happened in 2012, when anti-statehood leaders and some in Congress shamefully tried to nullify the sixty-one percent vote for statehood and reverse duly certified results by counting blank ballots as votes against statehood.

Idaho
1890 ★ The 43rd State

Once larger than Texas, Idaho was reduced by the advent of neighboring territories that became States. Lewis and Clark passed through, but its wilds saw little settlement until Mormons, thinking they were still in Utah, settled there in 1860.

The pilgrims' sanctuary was soon intruded upon as another gold rush brought the secular world into a clash of culture with Mormons. By 1863, the Congress adopted an organic act for territorial government based on the Northwest Ordinance tradition. Several years later as the population of Mormons and non-Mormons grew the territory developed toward statehood. The territorial regime sought to end the influence of Mormon theocracy by disenfranchising voters practicing polygamy. That policy was enshrined in the statehood constitution, overwhelmingly approved by a majority in 1889, not surprising since Mormons couldn't vote!

LESSONS FOR PUERTO RICO:

Internal regional tensions did not prevent citizens in Idaho from recognizing that statehood would be in the best interests of all. Like Hawaii, Wyoming, Arkansas and Florida, Idaho did not succumb to abstract legalistic rumination about whether Congress has to authorize a statehood constitution, and instead acted under the organic act to just get the job done.

Wyoming
1890 ★ The 44th State

Yet another Louisiana Purchase prize, Wyoming was the great natural cathedral of wonders, with a passage to the Pacific through which the Pony Express and transcontinental railway would pass. White encroachment was due to the railroads, and not another gold rush migration.

To address conflicts with persecuted Indian tribes fighting desperately for survival, territorial government was established by Congress in 1868. After developing habits of self-government in the Northwest Ordinance tradition in 1888, the local legislature petitioned Congress for a statehood-enabling act.

When Congress balked, a locally called convention adopted a statehood constitution that was voted on in 1889. Without undue partisanship, Wyoming was admitted in 1890. Wyoming became the first state to make suffrage a right of women.

LESSONS FOR PUERTO RICO:

Congress and the White House were controlled by Republicans after the 1888 elections. The territories of the Pacific Northwest were either Republican or the parties were roughly even. That had nothing to do with the constitutional principles governing admission, everything to do with the politics of admission.

Utah
1896 ★ The 45th State

Mormon pilgrims in 1847 migrated into Mexican lands that would soon become the Territory of Utah. In 1848, those lands were transferred to the U.S. under the Treaty of Guadalupe Hidalgo. A Mormon theocracy modeled after American government petitioned for statehood, but instead a territorial government based on the Northwest Ordinance model was established in 1850.

The head of the Mormon Church was appointed Governor, but between 1850 and 1894 it took seven constitutional conventions to adopt a statehood constitution on terms acceptable to Congress. Only after the Mormon hierarchy dissolved the political party it controlled and renounced the religion's practice of polygamy was Utah admitted as a State in 1896.

LESSONS FOR PUERTO RICO:

The U.S. Constitution does not establish an economic, religious or cultural order. Rather, it limits the powers of government and defines the rights of citizens. It reserves powers not granted to the government to the States, and citizens in each state adopt constitutions that limit the powers of State governments. Federal and State law can regulate economic and cultural matters subject to the limits of the Constitution.

As U.S. citizens living in a territory, the people of Puerto Rico currently have no power or right to limit the exercise of federal powers regulating cultural or economic issues in Puerto Rico.

Oklahoma
1907 ★ The 46th State

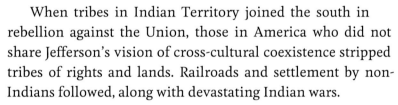

Thomas Jefferson, author of the Northwest Ordinance, envisioned a vast homeland for native tribes in the expanse of Louisiana Purchase lands to the west.

In 1828, five tribes were recognized as sovereign in greater Indian Territory, and progress of the Indian nations was promising. However, the practice of slavery brought out the worst in all Americans, including Indian tribes that profited from the slave trade and slave labor.

When tribes in Indian Territory joined the south in rebellion against the Union, those in America who did not share Jefferson's vision of cross-cultural coexistence stripped tribes of rights and lands. Railroads and settlement by non-Indians followed, along with devastating Indian wars.

In 1890, the Congress passed an organic act carving the Territory of Oklahoma from Indian Territory. Congress rejected admission of two States, one for the Indian tribes and the second the Territory of Oklahoma. Instead, under a 1906 enabling act, Indian Territory was merged with Oklahoma under a new constitution approved by voters, followed by admission in 1907.

LESSONS FOR PUERTO RICO:

The U.S. Constitution provided the framework for Americans to end slavery introduced by the British colonial empire and African slave traders. The price paid was immeasurably high for all peoples in our nation, including the Indian tribes.

No other nation embraces people of all ethnic origins more openly than America. That is why Louisiana, Oklahoma, New Mexico, Alaska and Hawaii are States.

New Mexico
1912 ★ The 46th State

After enduring Spanish and then Mexican militarism and colonial rule, the people of New Mexico became U.S. citizens under the 1848 treaty ending the U.S. war with Mexico. Congress acted promptly to pass a Northwest Ordinance model territorial organizing law in 1850.

For the next fifty years a series of inconclusive status resolution initiatives failed. By 1908, President Roosevelt, followed by Taft, gave politically opportunistic support to statehood for New Mexico.

New Mexico's political status fatigue made merger tolerable enough for approval in a 1906 vote, sponsored by Congress. Arizona rejected the merger.

In 1911, Congress enacted an enabling law for both Arizona and New Mexico. Taft caved in to Congressional meddling and vetoed the admission act to force politically gratuitous constitutional revisions.

LESSONS FOR PUERTO RICO:

Over eighty percent of New Mexico's residents spoke Spanish. The State constitution made Spanish and English official languages, not to ensure language equality for Spanish speakers, but for the minority that spoke English!

Language policy is a State rights issue under the 10th Amendment. Public schools in Puerto Rico should ensure bilingual proficiency, as private schools in the territory do now. The policy for Puerto Rico if Congress tries to force rather than support English education should be *"Don't tread on me!"*

Arizona
1912 ★ The 48th State

Also ceded to the U.S. in 1848, after two years of U.S. military administration, Congress adopted Arizona's first organic act in 1850.

Arizona was agitating for separate territory status based on its own Mexican border and Apache hostility. Under the slavery compromises of 1850, which had made admission of California possible, Arizona would have autonomy to decide the slavery issue as either a *separate territory or future State*. That led Arizona to adopt its own constitution and declare itself a State then send a delegate to the Confederate Congress during the Civil War. Union army occupation of Tucson elicited newfound loyalty to the U.S. and Congress rewarded Arizona with its own territorial organizing act, signed by Lincoln in 1862. A statehood constitution was approved in 1891, but partisan power brokers in Congress wanted to recombine Arizona with New Mexico or admit two states, depending on the shifting alignment of majority party control in Congress and the territories.

In 1910, Congress enabled a constitutional convention that adopted a voter approved State charter. After the imperious Taft officiously vetoed the admission act to force Arizona to amend its constitution's provision on removal of judges, admission was achieved in 1912.

LESSONS FOR PUERTO RICO:

Federal elections are like seasons, and a culturally diverse territory in which both national political parties are competitive needs to constantly read the seasonal climate conditions, and be as adaptive as the seasons are changeable.

Alaska
1959 ★ The 49th State

A decade after Alaska became a territory and U.S. citizenship was granted in 1867, 13 federal territorial bureaucrats were sent to govern 32,000 people in 586,000 square mile area. After the 1889 Klondike gold rush the population reached 62,000.

Under federal fishing, mining and shipping laws federal bureaucrats facilitated predatory exploitation of resources by politically influential special interests in New York, Washington, San Francisco and Seattle.

Corruption in the federal territorial government tainted President Taft in 1910, but reforms under a 1912 organic act were insufficient. Congress still imposed an appointed rather than elected Governor, and Washington had veto power over local laws.

Word War II, and the Cold War brought federal investment in infrastructure. Federal civilian and military presence along with increased self-government promoted a more stable civic order. Statehood would win voter approval by fifty-eight percent in 1946, sixty-eight percent in 1956, and eighty-three percent in 1958.

From 1950, when statehood gained momentum in Congress to 1959, when Alaska became a State, its Democratic majority among registered voters and Hawaii's majority of Republicans dominated Congressional jousting over linkage and de-linkage of admission bills for both territories.

Democrats in Congress outmaneuvered Eisenhower and the GOP by admitting Democrat Alaska before Republican Hawaii. The petty politics played by all concerned were gratuitous, especially since Hawaii has been Democrat and Alaska has been Republican since admission.

LESSONS FOR PUERTO RICO:

Congress knowingly neglected self-government and self-determination in Alaska, as it has in Puerto Rico. Alaska was a territory for 92 years, Puerto Rico is at 115 years and counting.

Cultural diversity and defining rights of citizenship for former non-citizens in territories were issues for Louisiana, New Mexico, Alaska, Hawaii and Puerto Rico. Only in Puerto Rico has Congress failed to recognize statehood as the proven way to integrate territorial people with U.S. citizenship into the nation.

49 Stars

Hawaii
1959 ★ The 50th State

Hawaii went from sovereign kingdom to a republic seeking annexation, and then became an incorporated territory populated by U.S. citizens.

Hawaii's integration into the federal Union required complex transitional measures, including a 1921 program to transfer the former Kingdom's lands to native Hawaiians. After 1934 Congress imposed tariffs on sugar from Hawaii that would not be allowed under statehood. The territorial legislature established the Hawaii Equal Rights Commission in 1935, soon to become the Hawaii Statehood Commission.

In 1940, a majority voted for statehood in a referendum sponsored by Congress. A statehood constitution was adopted in 1950, and in 1952 a joint Alaska-Hawaii statehood bill was filed in Congress.

Democrat and Republican platforms supported statehood for both territories, but Eisenhower and the GOP tried to stave off a Democratic takeover in Hawaii by enabling Republican leadership to deliver statehood before Democrat leaders in Alaska.

That backfires and Alaska is admitted first, followed by Hawaii, where ninety-four percent approve statehood in a final vote required by the admissions act.

LESSONS FOR PUERTO RICO:

Seeking to game the system for admission of a State based on short term and transient partisan self-interest is business as usual, until it becomes in effect anti-democratic. Both national political parties will be competitive in Puerto Rico when it is the 51st State, just as they have been during the territorial era.

Hawaii was annexed at a time when it was a foreign nation without native-born U.S. citizens. Like Louisiana, California, Alaska and New Mexico, in Hawaii the U.S. Congress made the decision to integrate most and eventually all non-citizen inhabitants fully into the American system of constitutional federalism through U.S. citizenship and statehood. Without rational basis, the U.S. has not yet made that decision in the case of Puerto Rico, even though that is the only permanent status possible other than separate nationhood and termination of U.S. citizenship.

The decision to admit a new State is a *political* question for Congress. However, if the results of Puerto Rico's 2012 referendum are confirmed in a follow-up vote, U.S. citizens in Puerto Rico will have met the same test Congress imposed on citizens in Hawaii. Hawaii precedent remains the obvious model for confirming consent to terms for admission prescribed by Congress.

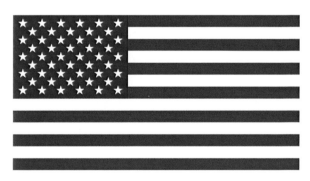

50 Stars

U.S. Flags Sampler:

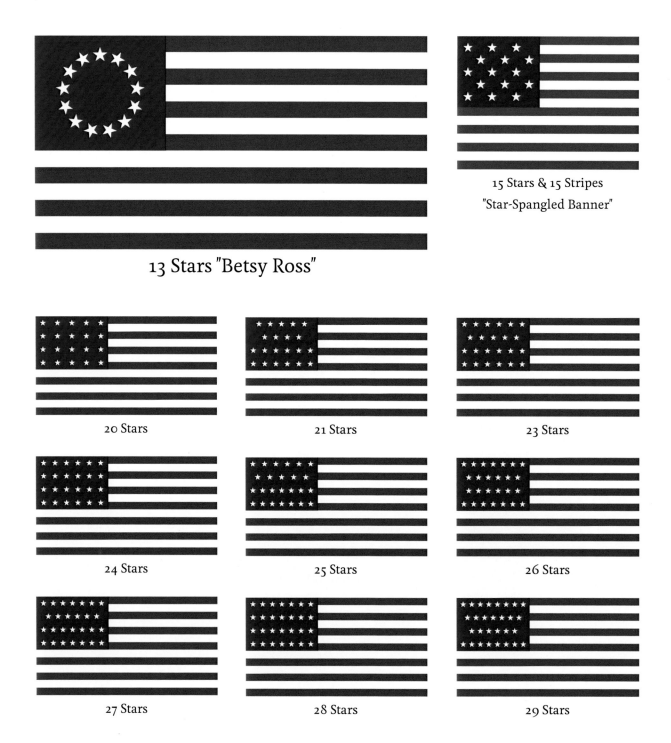

13 Stars "Betsy Ross"

15 Stars & 15 Stripes
"Star-Spangled Banner"

20 Stars

21 Stars

23 Stars

24 Stars

25 Stars

26 Stars

27 Stars

28 Stars

29 Stars

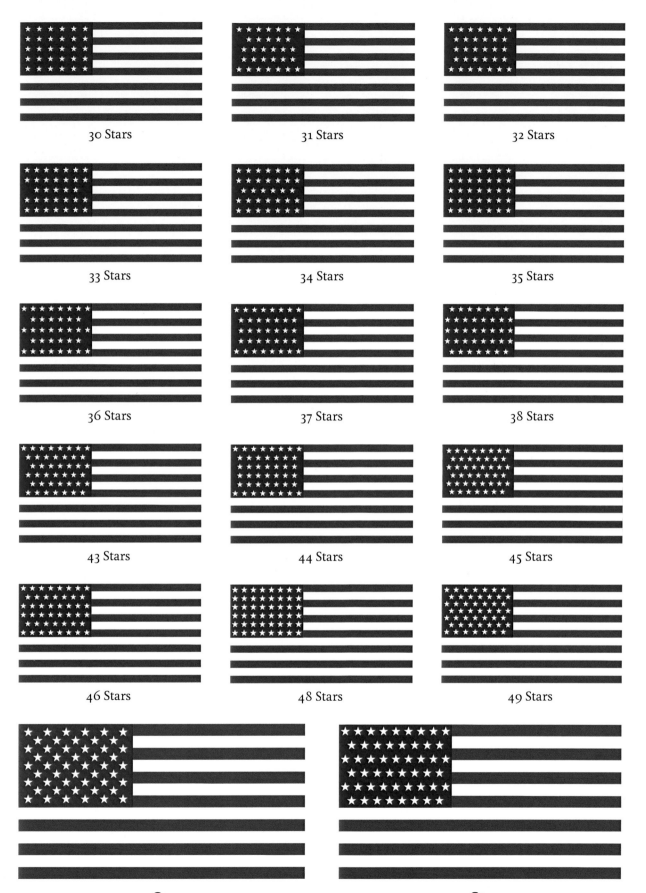

30 Stars

31 Stars

32 Stars

33 Stars

34 Stars

35 Stars

36 Stars

37 Stars

38 Stars

43 Stars

44 Stars

45 Stars

46 Stars

48 Stars

49 Stars

50 Stars

51 Stars

Selected Bibliography

Thornburgh, Dick. Puerto Rico's Future: A Time to Decide (with foreword by President G.H.W. Bush). Center for Strategic and International Studies (CSIS), Washington D.C. (2007)

Perkins, Whitney T. Denial of Empire: The United States and Its Dependencies. Leyden, The Netherlands: A.W. Sythoff (1962)

Grupo de Investigadores Puertorriquenos. Breakthrough from Colonialism: An Interdisciplinary Study of Statehood. Rio Piedras, Puerto Rico: Editorial de la Universidad de Puerto Rico (1984)

Hills, Howard L. Free Association for Micronesia and the Marshall Islands: A Transitional Political Status Model, 27 Hawaii L. Rev. 1 (2004)

About the Author

Howard L. Hills served in the Executive Office of the President, National Security Council and U.S. Department of State managing legal and diplomatic affairs in support of U.S. foreign policy and national security. He was lead counsel for the Reagan Administration for negotiation, ratification and implementation of political status treaties with Pacific island nations, securing military operating rights essential to President Reagan's missile defense and nuclear disarmament programs.

Hills also served as Vice President and General Counsel of the Overseas Private Investment Corporation, a specialized federal government owned public enterprise operating as an agency of the U.S. Department of State, promoting U.S. overseas private investment in support of American foreign policy and international development. Hills served as chief legal officer overseeing several billions of dollars annually in financial guarantees and political risk insurance to facilitate U.S. interests in 130 countries. Hills managed treaty relations, legal policy and Congressional affairs for the agency during its lead role in the U.S. response to the collapse of the former Soviet Union.

While on active duty as a U.S. Navy JAG officer for eight years, Hills served as Legal Counsel to the President's Personal Representative for Micronesian Political Status Negotiations. He also was designated Department of Defense Advisor for the National Security Council's Senior Interagency Group on Micronesian Political Status.

Hills became the Reagan Administration's lead counsel on territorial status policy in Congress, the federal courts and in U.N. Security Council proceedings. For military legal affairs service in support of national security Hills was awarded the Defense Superior Service Medal, Defense Meritorious Service Medal and Joint Services Commendation Medal.

Hills previously also served as a Peace Corps lawyer in the U.S. administered United Nations Trust Territory of the Pacific Islands, including the Federated States of Micronesia, Marshall Islands and Palau. After the Peace Corps he was appointed Deputy Legal Counsel to the House of Representatives in the Commonwealth of the Northern Mariana Islands, and Assistant Executive Director of the Guam Legislature's Law Revision Commission.

In his private legal career, Howard Hills was counsel in the Washington D.C. office of the New York based law firm Stroock, Stroock, Lavan. In 1996, he established the Law Office of Howard Hills.

Acknowledgements

As an international lawyer in the U.S. Navy JAG serving in the Executive Office of the President, and later as general counsel of a U.S. State Department agency, I witnessed firsthand the powerful impact of U.S. Attorney General Dick Thornburgh's intellectual as well as political leadership at the U.S. Department of Justice. On constitutional and treaty law issues related to American governed territories, I both served in support of and greatly admired his advocacy of sound federal legal policy.

It was, then, a true honor in 2003 when we collaborated to seek fully adequate compensation for the claims arising from U.S. nuclear testing in the Marshall Islands, and in researching his authoritative 2007 book on the history of U.S. territorial law. In these projects I once again saw firsthand that Thornburgh's legacy as a great American statesman is due not only to a brilliant legal mind, but in far greater part to the authenticity of his character and devotion to a life of service to our nation and humanity.

Accordingly, first and foremost I want to express my deep appreciation to Dick Thornburgh for his foreword framing the questions addressed in this book for readers. I also want to thank his colleague at the K&L Gates law firm, Glenn R. Reichardt, who over the years so patiently has mentored me in the skilled art of written advocacy. Both of these men generously volunteered their time to this project for no reason other than dedication to freedom and justice under the law of our land.

I also want to thank those true patriots in Puerto Rico— leaders in law and statesmanship—whose love for their island homeland and our nation made this project possible. It is an understatement to acknowledge that without their guidance and encouragement I could not have even attempted the task of adding the ideas in this book to the civic discourse, much less completed it.

Finally, I want to thank the original editor and publisher Craig Lockwood and book design artist Michael McCullen at Pacific Noir Pulp Press for a rewarding creative collaboration ennobled by a worthy purpose.